PROPHETIC HEALING

PROPHETIC HEALING:

HOWARD THURMAN'S VISION OF CONTEMPLATIVE ACTIVISM

BRUCE EPPERLY

Friends United Press
101 Quaker Hill Drive
Richmond, IN 47374 USA
info@fum.org
friendsunitedmeeting.org

Library of Congress Cataloging-in-Publication Data

Names: Epperly, Bruce Gordon, author.
Title: Prophetic healing : Howard Thurman's vision of contemplative
   activism / Bruce Epperly.
Description: Richmond, Indiana : Friends United Press, 2020. | Includes
   bibliographical references.
Identifiers: LCCN 2020014835 | ISBN 9780944350867
Subjects: LCSH: Thurman, Howard, 1900-1981. | Reconciliation--Religious
   aspects--Christianity. | Healing--Religious aspects--Christianity.
Classification: LCC BX6495.T53 E67 2020 | DDC 234/.131--dc23
LC record available at https://lccn.loc.gov/2020014835

Printed in the United States of America

CONTENTS

INTRODUCTION

A JOURNEY WITH HOWARD THURMAN

*The God of life is an adventurer
and those who would affirm their fraternity
must follow in His train.*[1]

Howard Thurman describes our relationship with God as a holy adventure. God is an adventurer who asks us to be adventurers, too! My vision of life as a holy adventure, which is also descriptive of my relationship with Howard Thurman, goes back nearly fifty years, when, as an undergraduate student at San Jose State University in California, I attended a lecture on spirituality and social change delivered by Thurman at Grace Baptist Church adjacent to the campus. Thurman was a guest of his longtime friend from the Fellowship of Reconciliation, an international peace organization, George L. "Shorty" Collins. At six feet, seven inches, "Shorty" towered over Thurman, but both men were spiritual giants, whose character and values have shaped my life, ministry, and writing ever since those conflict-ridden, Vietnam-era college days.

Now, nearly forty years after Thurman's death, I believe that his integration of spirituality and social transformation is more important than ever, as those of us who consider ourselves peacemakers seek to avoid the extremes of polarization and hopelessness in our confrontation with the apparently intractable social, economic, and political issues of our time. Like Thurman, we affirm the moral foundations of the universe and the presence of a divine providence moving through history orienting humankind toward God's Shalom, "a friendly world of friendly people," as Thurman says, embracing and affirming humankind in all its diversity. Yet we who describe ourselves as progressives or moderates easily succumb to anger and alienation in relationship to those who espouse views we find abhorrent. We easily condemn people as "deplorables," whose views we perceive as vastly different from ours in values, morality, and spiritual maturity. Despite our large-spirited theologies and political viewpoints, we often fall into the trap of "us" versus "them" in the same way the fundamentalists we decry separate the world into "saved" and "unsaved."

Today, perhaps more than ever before, we need people of great stature, like Howard Thurman, to help us reorient our spiritual GPS to chart the way through the wilderness of our twenty-first century cultural and religious chaos and conflict. Thurman shows us how to tap into resources greater than ourselves to face the machinations of the powers and principalities. In his own quest for spiritual stature to face the challenges of racism and social injustice, Thurman appreciatively quotes an unnamed poet in his *Deep Is the Hunger*:

> Each night my bonny, sturdy lad
> Persists in adding to his, Now I lay me
> Down to sleep, the earnest wistful plea:
> "God, make me big."
> And I, his mother, with greater need,
> Do echo in a humbled, contrite heart,
> "God, make me big."

Thurman adds his own interpretation of the poem, appropriate to the incivility and polarization of our time, as he notes that when we are presented with the opportunity to do something great for the world, too often we "cower in the presence of it. 'I can't do that. I am not equal to it.'" Or, as in the case of many privileged progressives like myself, "I am really not interested in it to that extent." Thurman confronts us:

"But there it is, and you have no available alternative but to tackle it. 'God make me big,' you cry out with all the power of your spirit. And then a strange thing happens. Strength comes from somewhere . . . . Deep within the task, something is released that eases the load; and the quality of your performance pervades your spirit with the assurance that God has answered. SO!"[2]

This is my prayer as I write this text. "God make me big!" I want to be a person of stature in my personal, spiritual, professional, and political life. I yearn to be strong enough to face the evils of twenty-first century North America. My desire is to follow the "better angels" of my nature, going from self-interest to world loyalty. The spiritual inclusiveness I seek to embody means embracing "otherness" in all its forms with a spirit of hospitality, despite great differences in politics and experience, and charity, despite the temptation to denigrate. I want this text to be "big" in its vision of human dignity and possibility.

I believe that this is your prayer as well. "God make us big" as we confront the maelstrom of our current political situation with courage and hope. We all have our "others" who fall out of our circle of compassion and respect: for some, it is Muslims, undocumented workers, immigrants, liberals, and the mainstream media; for others, it is members of white supremacy groups, conservative evangelicals, and fundamentalists. Despite our attempts to be inclusive and hospitable, we must confess that there are moments we succumb to the spirit of Psalm 139, a psalm whose honesty was dear to Thurman's heart.

> Do I not hate those who hate you, O Lord?
> And do I not loathe those who rise up against you?
> I hate them with perfect hatred;
> I count them my enemies. (Psalm 139:21–22)

Even the most irenic of us—and I seek to be a peacemaker, blessing everyone I meet—can feel a "holy hatred," a scathing judgmentalism far different from prophetic justice-seeking, toward those whose views and behaviors we oppose. Those whom we oppose become less than human in our estimation; the image of God within them is defaced and lost in our experience. But our quest for Shalom, wholeness, and peace will fail if we remain imprisoned by feelings of judgment and alienation. We need to find a path to righteous confrontation, speaking truth to power, that honors the holiness of those who appear to be "wholly other" to ourselves in politics, values, and lifestyle, even as we confront them on what we perceive to be unjust policies and actions. Like the psalmist, we discover the self we aspire to be in Thurman's vision of the "centering moment," by attending to the still, small voice of God:

> Search me, O God, and know my heart;
> test me and know my thoughts.
> See if there is any wicked way in me,
> and lead me in the way everlasting. (Psalm 139:23–24)

In recognizing that God knows us, we come to know ourselves and, then, align ourselves with God's all-inclusive vision. This sense of alignment with God's vision emerging in our social involvement can only happen when we tap the wellsprings of God's deep river of grace that flows into us during times of quiet prayer and committed self-transcendence.

This dynamic spirit of spiritual wholeness, joining contemplation and activism, is what I describe as prophetic healing. Prophetic healing involves our willingness to challenge the injustices of our time while maintaining a sense of God's presence in ourselves and in those with whom we contend in the political and social arenas. Prophetic healing reflects the profound sense of interdependence in which saint and sinner, and oppressor and oppressed, are ultimately joined in God's beloved community. The prophetic healer recognizes that healing must embrace all of us if it is to be lasting for any of us.

This text is inspired by my desire to join my spiritual aspirations to be a healer in every aspect of my life with creative and life-affirming social and political involvement. None of us is an innocent bystander. Each of us needs to find our pathway to justice-seeking and peacemaking, some through civil disobedience, others through picketing and phoning, still others through healing prayer. Although you might use different language to describe your spiritual aspirations, I suspect you are struggling with the same issue. My spirit is cumbered, as Quakers say, by angry comments on Facebook and Twitter, chaotic political leadership, and social media polarization. Some days, I am tempted to pick a fight with a "benighted" soul, whose social media comments I detest. At that moment, I realize that I must "center down" to find a path that empowers me to be politically active in ways that heal rather than harm, and unite rather than polarize. As Thurman counsels, I am—and I suspect you are—on a "search for common ground." In our time of binary thinking and political alienation, I believe that Thurman's wise vision can provide a pathway for contemplative activists and those who seek to bring their spiritual experiences to the task of healing the world. Our journey together will be one in which we ask God to make us big enough to be prophetic healers, whose persistent commitment to peace and justice transforms the world, our nation, our communities, our relationships, and ourselves.

The chapters to follow are a meditative dialogue between Howard Thurman and myself. Despite our differences in age, race, and privilege, we share a spiritual rhythm, grounded in our sense of the unity of all life as created and loved by God. We both affirm that we are on a holy adventure, with no guaranteed outcome, but with great trust in the "growing edge" of God's providential wisdom and love. We both seek a way to bring diverse viewpoints and political positions into a creative synthesis from which justice and peace may emerge. We both pray: "God make us big!" In eavesdropping on our dialogue, my prayer is that you discern your own path to committed spiritual and political transformation, with grace toward all and malice toward none.

Each chapter reflects a theme in Thurman's mystical-theological-prophetic journey as it relates to my own quest—and hopefully yours—to be God's companion in a process of prophetic healing. In the spirit of Thurman's pastoral spirituality, each chapter also concludes with a simple spiritual practice to illuminate our quest for prophetic healing. Along the way, we will hear the witness of other prophetic healers with whom Thurman was familiar, intellectually if not personally.

Inspired as I am by Thurman's contemplative activism, this text humbly represents *my* interpretation and creative synthesis of Thurman's insights. I am still on the road, and growing in my own spiritual stature, but I can affirm with feminist foremother Nelle Morton that "the journey is home." Wherever we are, God gives us sufficient wisdom and courage to face the challenges of joining spirituality and social activism.

As we begin this journey toward prophetic healing, I want to thank a holy trinity of mentors who touched my life and who themselves were good friends for over half a century, meeting initially through the Fellowship of Reconciliation, for their impact on my life: George L. "Shorty" Collins, Allan Armstrong Hunter, and Howard Thurman. In ways that I can't fully fathom, but for which I am deeply grateful, they shaped my ministry, writing, spirituality, and social concern. They live on in my commitment to personal and planetary healing.

"Shorty" provided my first opportunity to perform pastoral duties, as a long-haired college kid who had virtually no understanding of Christian theology but who, in the process of reading the scripture and singing hymns with a nursing home congregation, felt the first stirrings of my calling to be a preacher of the gospel. Allan Armstrong Hunter inspired college and graduate students like myself who attended the Claremont, California, Friends Meeting to "breathe the spirit in" contemplatively and "exhale" the spirit in social involvement. Howard Thurman has inspired me for nearly five decades through books that speak to my spirit in ways that nurture a creative synthesis of faith, compassion, and action. I want to thank those on the "front lines" who continue the long struggle for peace and justice, often against odds and from every faith tradition, including "none whatsoever," for their persistence in the quest for Shalom.

I am grateful to my editor Kristna Evans, who believed in this book and saw this as an important text to respond to the political polarization of our time. Finally, I want to thank my colleague at Georgetown University, Johanna Newberry Greene, a wise African American woman, two decades older than myself, who served as Associate Protestant Chaplain on my university ministry team, but was also often my mentor as she "channeled" the spirit of her own spiritual mentor Howard Thurman in her life and ministry.

This text is my humble and fallible attempt to find the right balance of head, heart, and hands to help secure a "friendly world of friendly persons" for my two young grandchildren, Jack and James, the Syrian refugee child, a Guatemalan toddler separated from her parents on the USA borderlands, the Appalachian miner's daughter, the inner-city bus driver's son, the dreamers from across the globe and the children of undocumented immigrants in the United States, and for children in every nation, so that laughter and love will characterize their days and joy and creativity will fill their hearts and minds. Let there be peace on earth and let it begin with us!*

— Epiphany 2020

Prophetic Healing in a Time of Protest and Pandemic

As this book was going to press, edited with page proofs being formatted, the world was rocked by the brutal murder of George Floyd at the hands of those whose calling is to protect and serve.

---

*A note on language, Howard Thurman did most of his writing prior to the concern for appropriately inclusive language in our descriptions of God and humankind. I have chosen, with a few exceptions, to follow his texts in their original form. I believe that Thurman would have updated his language, seeking creative ways to affirm and embrace the aspirations of all humankind, had he written at a later time.

The death of George Floyd unmasked in stark detail the American illusion of liberty and justice for all and the reality of structural racism already exacerbated in this time of pandemic. Howard Thurman knew racism and systemic racial violence first-hand. Thurman recognized that poverty and injustice stifled the human spirit.

Today, in the spirit of Howard Thurman, the Hebraic prophets and Jesus of Nazareth, protesting the realities of racism, police violence, and white privilege in daily life and the justice system is the only appropriate response for people of faith. We need prophetic healing in our nation. But this personal and systemic healing will only come after we repent America's original sins of slavery, racism, and the genocide of the First Americans.

Participating in the holy adventure Thurman envisaged for humankind must have at its heart an affirmation of diversity, a commitment to anti-racism, love of the earth, and preferential care for the most vulnerable. The moral and spiritual arcs of history bend long, and lean toward justice, but hope for personal and national transformation comes when we choose to push the moral and spiritual arcs forward as God's companions, God's hands and feet, in healing the earth. We protest and pray, knowing that God's vision of Shalom is the ultimate source of hope for persons and nations.

Thurman's dream of a beloved community of friendly persons in a friendly world still lures us forward. But we must begin to live the dream right where we, through contemplative activism that pickets and prays, and sees the dignity of all even as we affirm Black Lives Matter. This is the growing edge!

— August 2020

CHAPTER ONE

PROPHETIC HOPE IN THE MIDNIGHT HOUR

When the song of the angels is stilled,
When the star in the sky is gone,
When the kings and princes are home,
When the shepherds are back with their flock,
The work of Christmas begins:
To find the lost,
To heal the broken,
To feed the hungry,
To release the prisoner,
To rebuild the nations,
To bring peace among brothers,
To make music in the heart.[3]

Martin Luther King, Jr., once preached a sermon about a knock at midnight. In the course of his message, King asserted that it was midnight all over America: midnight in the social order, midnight in the psychological order, and midnight in the moral order. King's words were prophetic when first spoken in 1962, and they are surely prophetic today. If it isn't midnight in America, it appears that we are just a few moments away.

On January 14, 2018, on the eve of the celebration of Martin Luther King, Jr.'s, birthday, thousands panicked in the state of Hawaii as a false alarm, delivered over emergency communications, announced an imminent missile attack. Their panic was not ungrounded as the leaders of two nuclear powers called each other names, boasted of destroying one another, and compared the size of their nuclear arsenals like playground bullies.

Over the past few years my beloved homeland, the United States, has created fear and unrest across the globe through "America First" rhetoric and disengagement from global partnerships. The United States stands virtually alone in withdrawing from the Paris Climate Agreement, our leaders dismissing the preponderance of scientific data supporting the human impact on climate change and putting short-term profit over planetary well-being. Politicians brand entire ethnic groups as rapists and thugs and fan the flames of racial division. As King asserted, it is "midnight in our world, and the darkness is so deep that we can hardly see which way to turn."[4] In fact, it seems that business and political leaders are hell-bent on creating chaos and destruction. Yet on a dark night, for those who train their eyes toward the heavens in search of a wider perspective, the stars shine brighter and provide a pathway home.

Our world cries out for prophets who speak the truths the world may not want to hear and give us visions of what Howard Thurman regularly described as a "friendly world filled with friendly people," one of the anchor passages of this text. The dissonance between the concrete realities of our world and God's vision of Shalom is great. The prophetic calling to challenge the powerful, awaken the apathetic, give voice to the voiceless, and bring reconciliation to an increasingly polarized society, is daunting. In the spirit of the Hebraic prophets and Jesus, our quest is to see things from a God's eye view, seeking to midwife God's heavenly realm on earth as it is in heaven. We need prophetic healing, a strong commitment to justice grounded in the interplay of prayerful protest and equally prayerful reconciliation, as a people and as a nation.

Howard Thurman sought to be a prophetic healer. He recognized that we need to speak truth to power, confronting those who perpetrate injustice and destruction in the human and non-human worlds. His goal was to go beyond polarization to recognize the common identity we all share as God's children, despite profound differences in ethics and public policy, by embodying non-violent and reconciling responses toward those whose views or practices we oppose, without engaging in divisive power plays ourselves. He saw the goal of prophetic critique as including both oppressed and oppressor, seeking their ultimate reconciliation in the common ground of God's presence in all humankind. Thurman called on people who challenge injustice to ground their protest in reverence for God's presence in friend and foe alike.

The task of the prophetic healer is to pay attention to the signs of the times, reflected in the social order, the non-human world, the decisions of politicians and business leaders, and the quiet whisper of divine counsel. Prophetic healing seeks a pathway of social and political wholeness that binds together diverse communities, rich and poor, male and female, citizen and immigrant, left and right, and atheist and believer. The prophetic healer's word is always current and as contemporary as today's headlines. The prophetic word is also eternal in the sense that God's vision always joins the ongoing quest for Shalom, that Beloved Community in which humankind and the non-human world live in peace, with the seeds of creative transformation and healing sprouting in this present moment.

These are challenging days for prophets who experience God's call to speak unpleasant truths and present an alternative vision to the values and practices of our social order. Of course, then and now, the prophetic word shakes the complacent, rattles the powerful, and unnerves the prophets themselves. Just look at Isaiah and Amos and you will see the interplay of confidence and anxiety. Peer into the hearts of prophetic activists such as Oscar Romero, Desmond Tutu, Martin Luther King, Jr., Mahatma Gandhi, and Dorothy Day and you will glimpse them trying to balance courage and anxiety, divine companionship and solitary concern. They recognized their fallibility and limitations, and their own tendency to self-righteousness and exclusion, and yet with fear and trembling spoke the word of God, as they experienced it, to the social order of their time.

The prophetic word that comes to us today, as it did to Amos, Micah, Isaiah, and Jeremiah, is spoken with the backdrop of the growing gap between poor and rich, proliferation of hate crimes and racism, and planetary destruction. Inspired by their experience of God's pain at the suffering of the world, prophetic voices in every age challenge political and social practices that harm the vulnerable, even when harm is perpetrated by their own religious institutions. Today, we are their heirs!

Taking a page out of Israel in the time of Amos, prophetic critics challenge the court preachers of every era, religious leaders who praise unrestrained economic growth and inhospitality toward strangers. Prophetic voices of the eighth century BCE and our time denounce the behaviors of religious leaders who were willing to sell their spiritual integrity to support politicians sympathetic to their viewpoints. Drunk on political influence and entranced by their own justifications of wealth and power, the eighth-century court preachers and their descendants fail to hear the echoes of Amos' words: "Alas for you who desire the day of the Lord! Why do you want the day of the Lord? It is darkness, not light" for the nation and its leaders (Amos 5:18). To prophets then and now injustice has a cost personally and nationally. Our failure to seek justice and inability to hear the cries of the poor will lead not only to social chaos but our inability to experience God's call. In our time, we are still suffering as a nation from the wounds of slavery and our inability to affirm the equality of all people, men, women, people of color, and indigenous peoples.

Today the contemporary children of the court preachers, confronted by Amos, chant "Thank you, Jesus" and "God bless America" for gains in the stock market and their own personal prosperity even though the achievements they laud bring us closer to planetary doomsday. Identifying power, success, and prosperity with God's blessings, these proponents of the prosperity gospel and America-first ideologies are silent about injustice, preferring to focus on economic prosperity and narrow visions of "America's return to God." They applaud immigration policies that break up families, social mores that question the humanity of the LGBTQ+ community, and defend postures that threaten nuclear war, forgetting that Jesus welcomed outcasts and proclaimed "blessed are the peacemakers" (Matthew 5:9).

As we confront the evils of our time, we must humbly recognize that we are often guilty bystanders as well as social critics. We often fail to recognize the relationship between our intellectual, economic, and racial privilege and others' suffering. We are oblivious to our own complicity in injustice and planetary destruction because of our own lifestyles and investment in the economic status quo. We are unaware of the benefits we receive from business practices that put profits above people. Our false sense of innocence widens the gap and increases the division between ourselves and those whose policies we challenge, issuing in both polarization and hopelessness. Confessing our complicity in economic and social injustice delivers us from polarizing "us" versus "them" judgments. Recognizing the interplay of justice-seeking and complicity with injustice gives us both humility and hope.

On the one hand, it is easy for those of us who recognize the powers and principalities that confront us to give up hope in the future and, in our despair, exacerbate the polarization of our times. On the other hand, believing our cause to be right in comparison to the evils of others, we can succumb to the anger, vilification, and name-calling we denounce in those whose views we challenge. We become agents of division and deny the humanity of those whom we oppose through our own demeaning, denouncing, and dehumanizing. In affirming the humanity of the oppressed, we feel comfortable denying the humanity of those we perceive to be oppressors. At such times, we find inspiration in the words of prophetic healers, whose messages enable us to become prophetic healers ourselves.

The divisiveness of our time and the temptation to dehumanize our opponents mirrors the first days of Abraham Lincoln's presidency. Yet, Lincoln took the high road of spiritual maturity in his first inaugural address. Lincoln invoked the better angels of our nature, the quest for civility and compassion in a time of war, as an antidote to hatred for the perpetrators of injustice:

> Though passion may have strained it must not
> break our bonds of affection. The mystic chords
> of memory, stretching from every battlefield and
> patriot grave to every living heart and hearthstone

all over this broad land, will yet swell the chorus of
the Union, when again touched, as surely they will
be, by the better angels of our nature.[5]

Yet, still we ask: how do we put our "better angels" to work in
the quest for justice, human rights, and earth care when it seems as
if the powers and principalities know exactly what they are doing
in their promotion of xenophobia, racism, greed, and planetary destruction? Can we forgive them when they purposely promote divisiveness and turn their backs on planetary well-being? Can we, who
affirm "reverence for life," expand the circle of reverence to include
those whose political policies we challenge? Can we maintain our
spiritual center while protesting injustice, when protest is identified
by those we challenge as unpatriotic and when any sense of national
unity or recognition of the "loyal opposition" appears to be disinte-
grating due to incivility and polarization?

In the midst of the enveloping gloom, we look for hope in the
growing edges of grace that enable us to speak and act for justice
while trusting that God is present and moving in the lives of those
who perpetuate injustice. In crying out against injustice, we yearn
for faith that hearts of stone can be softened with compassion. In the
midnight hour, King believes that we can find "faith in the dawn."

> Faith in the dawn arises from the faith that God is
> good and just. When one believes this, he knows
> that the contradictions of life are neither final nor
> ultimate. He can walk through the dark night with
> the radiant conviction that all things work together
> for good for those who love God. Even the most
> starless midnight may herald the dawn of some
> great fulfillment.[6]

In this time of midnight in America and expanding gloom across the planet, we need models in our quest for prophetic healing. We need images of prophetic action that heals rather than destroys. We find such images in South Africa's Truth and Reconciliation Commission, following the fall of apartheid, peacemaking programs that bring together Israeli and Palestinian youth, and conservatives and progressives who look for common ground in responding to unemployment, homelessness, and reducing the frequency of abortion while promoting women's equality. We also experience hope for transformation in the commitments of young people like Greta Thunberg and the Parkland, Florida, high school students, who go beyond self-interest to work for the health and safety for future generations.

Hope comes when we get off our couches and support those who are victims of discrimination and climate injustice. By our own dedication to prophetic healing, we may become images of hope to others when we build bridges to people with different political viewpoints or bring together people from diverse ideological, religious, or ethnic communities. Transformation comes when we fight the good fight for justice and planetary healing, challenging the powers and principalities, while affirming our common dignity as brothers and sisters, created in God's image.

I believe that the spiritual vision of twentieth-century African American mystic Howard Thurman provides a pathway to healing in a time of national division. Thurman spoke on behalf of those whose backs were against the wall. He knew what it was like to be second class and at the mercy of forces determined to preserve white supremacy and turn back the clock to antebellum America. As a youth he knew that, at any moment, he could be cited for "driving while black"* or verbally abused as ignorant by someone far less educated than himself.

Whites could travel safely and confidently through black neighborhoods in Thurman's Daytona, Florida, while African Americans were suspect whenever they crossed Daytona's color line into white enclaves. Thurman knew from the inside out the temptation to vilify, hate, demean, and destroy those who oppress the vulnerable and those who diminish our lives for the sake of power and profit. Yet Thurman also knew that violence, bullying, name-calling, and demeaning of opponents destroys the spirits of all who use these tactics, regardless of power or position in society, or lack thereof.

Thurman often wrote to those he described as "apostles of sensitiveness," people of privilege who sought to protest prayerfully as well as assertively, recognizing that God is present in our quest to create a pathway from society's injustice to the achievement of a just, equitable, and compassionate social order. He urged them to listen to the voices of the voiceless as they heard their own unuttered cries for authentic relationships. He also counseled them to hear God's voice in the knee-jerk racist and political demagogue.

Thurman's sense of divine providence moving through history, driving humanity as a whole forward toward justice despite the machinations of the powerful called him to a higher path than violence, polarization, incivility, and alienation. Thurman proposed a liberation spirituality based on bringing our sense of unity with God and our essential human dignity—and the human dignity of

---

* A parody of the term driving while intoxicated, this phrase refers to the idea that a motorist can be pulled over by a police officer simply because they are black and then charged with a trivial or perhaps non-existent offense. (Source: www.urbandictionary.com)

all people—to our responses to the political and social crises of our time. Thurman possessed the prophetic vision of an alternative reality to the unjust social order and this vision included the vision of a transformed world in which oppressor and oppressed would let go of their social and economic locations in the quest for common ground and social change. In the words of Martin Luther King, Jr., whose own quest for peaceful social transformation was influenced by Thurman:

> I have a dream that one day on the red hills of
> Georgia, sons of former slaves and sons of former
> slave owners will be able sit down together at the
> table of brotherhood . . . I have a dream that one
> day, down in Alabama, with its vicious racists . . .
> little black boys and black girls will be able to join
> hands with little white boys and white girls as
> sisters and brothers.[7]

God calls us to be dreamers, not conformed to this world. As the Apostle Paul counsels, we should be constantly transformed by the renewing of our hearts and minds. (Romans 12:2) As we dream of a new heaven and new earth, we can, despite our apparent powerlessness, choose to become citizens of a world that is yet to come, the world God imagines for us.

As those who seek to become prophetic healers, we must join our quest for justice with compassion and, despite external conflict, remember that the ultimate goal of prophetic critique is the healing of both people and the social order. Our goal is to move from polarization to common ground, motivated by the dream of God's beloved community in which diversity leads to dialogue and multiplicity inspires creative transformation. This quest, as Thurman asserts, is the growing edge of hope that enables us to persevere as we face the evils of our time.

Look well to the growing edge!
All around us worlds are dying
and new worlds are being born;
All around us life is dying and life is being born.
The fruit ripens on the tree;
the roots are silently at work in the darkness of the earth
against a time when there shall be new leaves,
fresh blossoms, green fruit.
Such is the growing edge!
It is the extra breath from the exhausted lung,
the one more thing to try when all else has failed,
the upward reach of life when weariness
closes in upon all endeavor.
This is the basis of hope in moments of despair,
the incentive to carry on when times are out of joint
and men have lost their reason, the source of confidence
when worlds crash and dreams whiten into ash.
The birth of the child—
life's most dramatic answer to death—
this is the growing edge incarnate.
Look well to the growing edge![8]

A PRACTICE FOR PROPHETIC HEALING

We need to become dreamers, visualizing alternative realities to our current unjust and violent national ethos. We also need to remember, with Thurman, that change begins with us. Our vocation is to change our hearts and minds and expand our imaginations to embrace friend and foe alike. As we pay attention to God's presence in our lives and our own temptation to incivility and polarization, we begin to see the world with eyes of love not fear, reconciliation not alienation.

First, let us begin with a contemplative practice I learned from Thurman's close friend and colleague, Allan Armstrong Hunter:

> I breathe the Spirit deeply in
> And blow it peacefully out again.

Take a few moments, letting God's Spirit fill you from head to toe, giving you a sense of peace and safety. Allow your breathing to center you in God's Great Breath, flowing through you and all creation, including those with whom you contend. Then reflect prayerfully on the questions: Who are my "others?" Who do I look down upon? Who are objects of my judgment or derision? In recognizing the importance of healing our attitudes, we take important steps in healing the world. In that spirit, pause to pray for the objects of your alienation. With each breath, visualize God's love surrounding them and giving them wisdom and calm.

In this spiritual self-awareness practice, I identified my own sense of judgment toward those national leaders whose political policies are an anathema to me as well as those who, from my perspective, blindly and uncritically follow them. In that spirit, I have made a commitment to pray daily for those whose political stances I oppose, asking that God's wisdom and compassion flow into their lives and families as well as my own.

Second, as a matter of spiritual self-awareness, I have made a daily commitment to 1) regularly examine my own judgmentalism, insensitivity, temptation to solve problems violently, 2) to recognize personal imperfection, confessing my sin and asking for God's mercy and a conversion of heart, and 3) to become more aware of my privileges of race, economics, and education. This is a matter of spiritual self-awareness rather than guilt, believing that recognition is the first step to personal transformation and growth in empathy. I often say, in the words of Psalm 139, "Search me, and know me" or repeat a version of the Jesus Prayer, "Lord, have mercy upon me. Lord, have mercy upon me. Lord, have mercy upon me" as I open to divine grace and wisdom. In seeking self-awareness each morning and evening and throughout the day, I find a quiet center that calms my fears and gentles my attitudes.

CHAPTER TWO

CONTEMPLATIVE ACTIVISM AND ACTIVE CONTEMPLATION

*The mystic is forced to deal with social relations
because, in his effort to achieve the good,
he finds that he must be responsive to the
human need by which he is surrounded, particularly
the kind of human need in which the sufferers are
victims of circumstances over which, as individuals,
they have no control; circumstances that are not
responsive to the exercise of an individual will,
however good and however perfect.*[9]

Howard Thurman has been one of my spiritual and theological heroes for over four decades. I first encountered him in the 1970's. Not unlike today, the times were turbulent. The Vietnam War was raging and there was violence in the streets. Racial tensions were high as people of color sought liberation from the impact of centuries of racism, powerlessness, and white privilege. Cesar Chavez and the farm workers marched for dignity and economic justice. There were signs of presidential abuse of power that foreshadowed the Watergate break-in, eventual cover-up, and impeachment of Richard Nixon.

In the maelstrom of social upheaval, Thurman spoke softly and slowly about his spiritual journey, social activism, and its relevance to the war in Vietnam. He chose his words carefully, but beneath the calm, there was a call to a contemplative activism that was rare in those times of political and social polarization. Whatever changes we seek, Thurman counseled, must be grounded in a process of centering down, which opens us to the still, small voice of divine guidance in our personal and political lives and enables us to see the divinity in those whose behaviors and policies we oppose. Thurman asserted that our protests become prayers when they are grounded in our experience of God's light in ourselves and those whom we challenge.

A few years after my initial encounter, I heard Thurman give a series of lectures at Scripps College in Claremont, California. Once again, Thurman spoke with depth and deliberation about the spiritual journey as it related to the lives of professors and students. I felt a spiritual kinship with this aging African American spiritual guide. We were both contemplatives, committed to the practices of prayer and meditation. We were both more at home in the study, classroom, and pulpit than on the picket lines, but both of us knew that reflection without action contributes little to the healing of the earth. My sense of kinship grew as I read virtually the entire corpus of Thurman's work as a graduate and seminary student at Claremont Graduate School and Claremont's Disciples Seminary Foundation.

Although both of us preferred writing and teaching to picketing and protesting, we shared a common recognition that authentic scholarship and ministry compel us to claim the prophetic mantle in response to structural and political violence and injustice. Solitary hours of contemplation find their fulfillment when we claim our role as God's companions in healing the world. Spiritual practices give us perspective to transcend polarization and patience to persist in the quest for justice despite the slow movements of the moral arc of history. Times of quiet meditation enable us to experience the inner spirit of God in all people—and beyond humankind—and search for ways to discern divinity in those who seek to be our enemies.

I admired Thurman for his equanimity, inner strength, and commitment to follow in the footsteps of the One who challenged his followers to love their enemies. I appreciated his quiet, behind-the-scenes mentoring of civil rights leaders such as Martin Luther King, Jr., Vernon Jordan, Bayard Rustin, and Jesse Jackson. Although few spoke of white privilege at the time, I came to realize that, despite my family's modest means, I had been born into privilege as a result of my race and parents' education. Thurman also came from modest means, but, in contrast to my experiences as a Bay Area "hippie" only occasionally harassed by the police, Thurman dealt with racism every day of his life.

In spite of his accomplishments, Thurman knew what it was like to have his "back against the wall," the experience of oppression and challenges to his self-worth by the overt racism of Jim Crow laws and subtle racism of white privilege and entitlement. Still, Thurman persisted in seeking common ground with those who judged him to be inferior primarily by the color of his skin. Thurman believed with the Quaker tradition that there was "something of God" in a fearful and angry Klansman that hate could not destroy. Hate and sin were real and could destroy the spirit, but deeper than institutional racism was the original wholeness, described in the Genesis affirmation of the image of God present in each woman and man. Like the jagged geode, each of us possesses an inner beauty, the divine center, despite our hardened exteriors. If we awaken to our inherent holiness and the holiness of our brothers and sisters, oppressor and oppressed alike can experience the healing power of reconciliation.

When I first met Thurman, what impressed me most about him was his spiritual depth and calm demeanor. Yet his quest for God was far from individualistic or passive. Thurman affirmed that the breath of creation, the pulse of divinity he first experienced on the beaches and in the woodlands of Daytona, Florida, was present in all creation, enlivening every creature. With the Apostle Paul, he recognized that God was the reality "in whom we live and move and have our being" (Acts 17:28). This same divine wisdom and energy is present, albeit often unrecognized, in both the segregationist and protestor, immigration officer and undocumented worker, manipulative politician and community organizer. If there is any hope of reconciliation, we must embrace our better angels and higher selves, enabling us to spiritually join those who once were opponents and enemies in the search for the common good of community, nation, and planet.

As he reflected on marching with Martin Luther King, Jr., the Jewish theologian and mystic Abraham Joshua Heschel recalled that he felt like his legs were praying. I found that same prayerful journey to justice in Howard Thurman. I saw in Thurman the affirmation that I could be both "heavenly minded and earthly good." Thurman modeled the interplay of deep prayer and wise political involvement. He embodied spiritual practices that joined head, heart, and hands to bring healing to congregations, communities, and the world. In his ministry and teaching, Thurman pointed the way to a politics of reconciliation that holds the promise of creative conversation, mutual respect, and common cause between people of contrasting political viewpoints and diverse life experiences.

Now more than ever these spiritual practices are needed as we are daily bombarded by one crisis after another. In the course of every day, I receive dozens of headlines on my internet news feeds, most of which are disheartening in their reports of gun violence, sexual harassment by celebrities and political leaders, disregard for civility at the highest levels, nuclear escalation, and intentional environmental destruction. Without contemplative practices, we burn out, lash out in anger, or give up hope. In finding our depth and the original wholeness hidden in our perception of others, we reclaim our spiritual GPS and find new energy in our quest for Shalom. This was Thurman's vision and our hope as contemplative activists today.

A PRACTICE FOR PROPHETIC HEALING

Take time in the days ahead to reflect with your whole self on the wisdom of Psalm 46:

> God is our refuge and strength,
> a very present help in trouble.
> Therefore we will not fear,
> though the earth should change,
> though the mountains shake
> in the heart of the sea;
> though its waters roar and foam,
> though the mountains tremble with its tumult.
> There is a river whose streams
> make glad the city of God,
> the holy habitation of the Most High.
> God is in the midst of the city;
> it shall not be moved;
> God will help it when the morning dawns.
> The nations are in an uproar, the kingdoms totter;
> he utters his voice, the earth melts.
> The Lord of hosts is with us;
> the God of Jacob is our refuge.
> Come, behold the works of the Lord . . .
> He makes wars cease to the end of the earth;
> he breaks the bow, and shatters the spear;
> he burns the shields with fire.
> "Be still, and know that I am God!

I am exalted among the nations,
I am exalted in the earth."
The Lord of hosts is with us;
the God of Jacob is our refuge.

Begin your time of reflection with a period of five to ten minutes of silence. You may choose simply to quietly wait on God's wisdom. You may also choose to focus on your breath or use a simple repetitive phrase, such as "Be still" or "I breathe the Spirit deeply in." Then read the passage slowly twice, focusing on its meaning in your life. What words or phrases address your condition? Where do you experience stillness in the chaos? Where do you find God's wisdom and faithfulness in the maelstrom of political conflict? Close with a prayer for divine guidance in your response to social and political issues.

Return throughout the day to this experience of still-ness, seeking to deeply breathe in God's Spirit, and reciting the words, "Be still and know that I am God," as you seek to experience God's peace flowing through all creation, friend and foe alike. If, in the course of the day you begin to ex-perience anxiety at the news or a sense of alienation and judgment in relationship to those with whom you disagree theologically or politically, return to your breath, breathing deeply the peace of God that calms and empowers.

CHAPTER THREE

THURMAN'S MYSTICAL JOURNEY

I could sit my back against its trunk, and feel the
same peace that would come to me in my bed
at night. I could reach down in the quiet places
of the spirit, take out my bruises and my joys,
unfold them, and talk about them. I could talk aloud
to the oak tree and know that I was understood.
It, too, was part of my reality, like the woods,
the night, and the pounding surf, my earliest
companions, giving me space.[10]

Thurman's childhood and youth were challenging to say the least, both culturally and spiritually. Born in Daytona, Florida, in 1899, the grandson of slaves, Thurman was well aware of the trauma of discrimination. Thurman grew up in the era of Jim Crow laws and voter suppression. Thurman experienced white supremacy on a daily basis, not just among the obviously racist members of the Ku Klux Klan, but in the pervasive, unreflective racism, characteristic even of those whites who sought to be friendly to the black community.

An incident from Thurman's youth captures the ubiquitous reality of racism he and most southern African Americans daily experienced. One autumn Thurman was hired to rake the leaves of a family that had employed his grandmother to do their laundry for many years. As he raked, their young daughter, perhaps four or five, would playfully scatter piles of leaves that contained colorful leaves she wanted to show Howard. When Howard became frustrated and told her to quit, and then threatened to tell her father when she continued to scatter the leaves, she angrily poked him with a hat pin. In response, Howard drew back, exclaiming in pain, eliciting her comment, "O Howard, that didn't hurt you! You can't feel!"[11] That child's unreflective comment betrayed many whites' assumption that African Americans were somehow subhuman, unable to feel the pain inflicted upon them in the cotton fields of slavery and the antebellum separation of families and in the twentieth-century exclusion from soda fountains, voting booths, and playgrounds. Embedded in relational and legal realities of southern white privilege was the dehumanization of people of color, reflected in the belief that people of color were only slightly superior to the beasts of the fields. If you can't feel, then you are subhuman and undeserving of respect or ethical consideration, even from devout white Christians. Later, Thurman was to see empathy, the ability to identify with another's feelings, along with the affirmative reverence for life, grounded in the image of God residing in all people, as essential to racial equality and social justice.

The social and economic structure of the South stifled the dreams of people of color. Education was considered a luxury for black youth and during Howard's youth Florida provided few opportunities to a bright young black person to advance educationally. Teenage Howard Thurman found out there were only three public high schools for black youth in the state of Florida. Thurman learned early that "separate but equal" is inherently unequal. One of the greatest injustices of racism, Thurman was later to assert, was its stunting of the imagination of budding children and youth. Sadly, the historical impact of slavery and legal discrimination still shapes the lives of many inner city youth for whom the realities of gangs and teen pregnancy often displace prospects for higher education, professional success, and spiritual fulfillment. This same tragic stunting of the spirit is also found among Kurdish and Somalian refugees in camps, Appalachian children of unemployed mine workers, girls who are told what they *can't* do as a result of their gender, and "dreamers," children of undocumented parents, uncertain of their future in the United States. In contrast to many youths of his time and ours, Thurman was fortunate to have a mother and grandmother who nurtured his dreams and affirmed his inherent value as a child of God. These courageous women constantly reminded him that he was "somebody" regardless of what southern whites thought of him.

From the very beginning of his life, young Thurman had a mystic sense. He felt the universe as one great pulse of Divine Love. He felt at one with the winds and sea. "When I was young," Thurman recalls, "I found more companionship in nature than with people . . . . The quiet, even the danger, of the woods provided my rather lonely spirit with a sense of belonging that did not depend on human relationships."[12] Young Thurman discovered that we live in an enchanted universe in which every creature can praise God just by being itself (Psalm 150:6). In the enchanted reality Thurman experienced as a youth and throughout his life, all things reveal divinity and are of value, oak tree and black teenager alike. God speaks in our cells as well as our souls, and trees, woodlands, and seashores can become what the Celtic Christians described as "thin places" through which God is revealed to us. As a child, Thurman gained a sense of the spiritual unity of all things, grounded in the experience that "all things were one lung all of life breathed . . . a vast rhythm enveloping all, but I was a part of it and it was a part of me."[13]

Organized religion and its doctrinal beliefs were both inspiring and problematic for young Thurman. Although Howard's mother and grandmother were devout Baptists, his grandmother, a former slave, asked Howard not to read certain passages from the Apostle Paul's writings, asserting that these same writings were used by her "owner" to justify his and other slaveowners' divine right to possess their slaves. He knew that religion could be a balm in Gilead, but it could also kill the spirit and deaden dreams.

Howard Thurman experienced both the pettiness and grandeur of his childhood religion. On the one hand, young Howard saw through narrow orthodoxy and religious exclusivism. When his father, a good but agnostic man, died, their Baptist pastor would not conduct his funeral or allow him to be buried in the church yard. They finally found a minister willing to preach at his father's funeral. Thurman recalls being spiritually traumatized by the itinerant evangelist's perorations, "I listened with wonderment, then anger, and finally mounting rage as Sam Cromarte preached my father into hell."[14] At that moment, Howard vowed never to have anything to do with the church. While Howard's vow was short-lived, that experience shaped his theology and spirituality. He realized that spirituality, and even orthodox religion, is not about abstract doctrines but the concrete experiences of fallible, wonderful, questioning, believing, ambiguous flesh and blood people, and that even includes ministers. If you believe in a loving God, you have to walk the talk in your affirmation of God's presence in all of life's cultural, racial, and spiritual others. Questions, along with diverse expressions of faith, deepen rather than destroy our commitment to God.

Despite its theological limitations, young Howard gained a sense of self-worth in the Baptist church of his youth. "Looking back, it is clear to me," Thurman affirmed, "that the watchful attention of my sponsors in church served to enhance my consciousness that whatever I did in life mattered." To bolster young Howard's spirit, his grandmother would share stories from her days as a slave. Howard remembers his grandmother describing the words of a slave preacher to the gathered slave community of which she was a part. After preaching about Christ's death on Calvary, he would pause and then proclaim, "You are not niggers! You are not slaves! You are God's children!"[15] Variations of this same affirmation inspired Thurman to believe that the limitations white society and rule of law placed on him were not reflective of God's vision and his inherent worth as a beloved child of a Loving Creator.

The radical affirmation that each person possesses an inner light, something of the divine, inspired Thurman's dream of a benevolent universe characterized by friendly and affirmative people. Deep faith is global, not parochial, and salvation and revelation are offered to humankind as a whole despite its diversity of belief systems, faith perspectives, and rituals. In reflecting on the spiritual malpractice perpetrated by the preacher at his father's funeral, I believe that Thurman would have appreciated Paul Tillich's insight that doubt is an essential component of faith and that orthodoxy without compassion, as the Apostle Paul notes, is like a noisy gong or clanging cymbal. In the spirit of John's gospel, Thurman came to believe that "the true light, which enlightens everyone, was coming into the world" (John 1:9).

Looking back on his childhood, Thurman recalls the origins of his lifelong sense of divine providence moving in and through all things emerging in response to the appearance of Halley's Comet in 1910. The amazing spectacle elicited apocalyptic fears in Howard's neighborhood. Some of his neighbors even purchased "comet pills" to provide protection from the conflagration that would occur when the comet struck the earth. A frightened eleven year old, Thurman asked his mother, "What will happen to us if that thing falls from out of the sky?" With a sense of radiant peace that transformed fear into trust, she responded, "Nothing will happen to us, Howard. God will take care of us."[16] In life and death, in peace and conflict, Thurman discovered that God is with us, sustaining and guiding our personal adventures. As I write these words on a cold Cape Cod winter day, we are in the heart of Kwanzaa, and people of all ethnic backgrounds can appreciate the Kwanzaa affirmations, inspired by the spirit of African harvest celebrations: unity, self-determination, collective work and responsibility, collective economics, purpose, creativity, and faith. Thurman recognized that God's wisdom inspired African religions and the faith of slaves as well as the Galilean vision of Jesus and the religion that sprung from Jesus' teachings.

The power of the negro spirituals inspired and energized Thurman throughout his life. Thurman believed that the genius of the slave preachers and song writers is still alive today in those who march for justice and challenge hate in its obvious and subtle forms, mostly hate perpetuated by those who claim to be Jesus' followers: "By some amazing but vastly creative spiritual insight the slave undertook the redemption of a religion that the master had profaned in his midst."[17] In the spirit of the antebellum, nineteenth-century slave preachers, Thurman sought to share the insight that despite the limitations of racism and injustice, "every human being was a child of God. This belief included the slave as well as the master."[18] Though often hidden by fear and anger, God is present in every person regardless of race, social standing, or political perspective. God is present in the least of these as well as those who seek to perpetuate injustice and violence to maintain their place in the social order. Today, we would extend Thurman's example to include white supremacists marching in Charlottesville, Virginia, bombers of synagogues and churches, and politicians who roll back civil liberties and protection of the environment.

Thurman's calling was to see and then bring forth awareness of God in its most unlikely places. That is our calling today, to become God's companions in healing the world, so that our prophetic actions will reconcile rather than divide and transform rather than destroy the communities in which we live. While there is no "one way" to follow Jesus or one absolute doctrinal path to understand Jesus, the clear and obvious way of Jesus travels the road of hospitality, love, healing, and inclusion. Transformation comes through God's grace, the power that changes lives and enables us to face hatred with courage, grace, persistence, and power.

A PRACTICE FOR PROPHETIC HEALING

For this chapter's practice I invite you to read Maya Angelou's poem, "The Pulse of the Morning," initially delivered at the Inauguration of President William Jefferson Clinton in 1983.[19] It echoes the pulse of life that Thurman felt as he laid his back against that noble oak tree and concludes with words that Thurman could have written: after looking at our brother's or sister's faces, knowing that earth, sky, water, and wind, as well as humankind is kin, we speak simply, "with hope / Good morning."

After reading Angelou's poem, available online and in the poet's own anthologies, you might take a copy of it with you to read meditatively at various times in the days ahead. As you reflect on Angelou's poem throughout the next few days, find a place of beauty, your sacred space, and spend several days simply experiencing the pulse of life flowing in and through you. Experience your connection to the four primordial elements—air, earth, fire, and water—and the environment around you. Feel God's presence in the flora and the fauna, and the breeze, sunlight, or rain. In human sounds, listen for divine melodies. Experience yourself saying "good morning" to creation with each new day. Praise and give thanks to the One in whom all live, move, and have their being.

CHAPTER FOUR

THE EDUCATION OF A CONTEMPLATIVE ACTIVIST

*There can be no cultivation of the mind,
no opening of the heart to the living spirit
of the living God, no raw laceration of the nervous
system created by the agony of human suffering,
pain, or tragedy; there can be no thing that
does not have within it the signature of God,
the Creator of life, the living substance out of which
all particular manifestations of life arise;
there is no thing that does not have within it
as part of its essence, the imprimatur of God,
the Creator of all, the Bottomer of existence.* [20]

Howard Thurman believed that divine providence moves through our lives making a way where we perceive no pathway forward. God comes to us in mystical experiences, insights, and synchronous encounters, just as God appeared in the lives of the biblical patriarchs and matriarchs, Hebraic prophets, and Jesus' first followers. Everywhere God is at work seeking wholeness and awakening us to our inner light, especially in times of despair and conflict.

Thurman believed that God's providential care enabled him to attend a high school in Florida, when at the time only three schools in the whole state were open to African American students, the nearest being in Jacksonville, almost a hundred miles away from his home in Daytona Beach. To attend high school, Howard would have to live with one of his cousins. When he attempted to board the train to move to Jacksonville, the railroad official refused to let him put his cumbersome and dilapidated trunk on the train. He would have to send his trunk "express," but lacked the money necessary for the transaction. Defeated and fearing that he would not be able to continue his education, Thurman sat on the curb and began to cry. Out of nowhere, a shabbily dressed African American man appeared, asking him "What the hell are you crying about?" When Howard shared his lament, the stranger responded, "If you're trying to get out of this damn town to get an education, the best I can do is help you." He marched Thurman up to the office, paid the fee, and disappeared without a word.[21] There are truly times when we entertain angels unaware (Hebrews 13:2), who provide us with what we need at the exact time we need it!

Thurman believed that providence surely was at work in his attending Morehouse College, an historically black college, where he received not only a world-class education, but also a sense of dignity that transcended the indignities African Americans routinely experienced. His sense of self was deepened by his encounter with Morehouse's president John Hope, who was the mouthpiece of God's affirmation to an anxious young man.

> He always addressed us as "young gentlemen."
> What this term of respect meant to our faltering
> egos can only be understood against the backdrop

of the South of the 1920's. We were black men
in Atlanta during a period when the state of
Georgia was infamous for its racial brutality.
Lynchings, burning, unspeakable cruelties were the
fundamentals of existence for black people. Our
physical lives were of little value. Any encounter
with a white person was inherently dangerous
and frequently fatal. Those of us who managed to
remain physically whole found our lives defined in
less than human terms.[22]

In a time in which black men of all ages were addressed as "boy"
or "uncle" and women as "Mary," President Hope reminded Thurman and his fellow students that the image of God shined through
the gloom of racism and that the light of God could not be extinguished by the diabolical spirit of white supremacy. Thurman's world
opened up. Not limited by race or economics, he could imagine great
things and then achieve them by God's grace.

Following graduation from Morehouse, Thurman became one
of three African American students admitted to Rochester Theological Seminary, where for the time he found himself living in a
totally white world. Sadly, he also discovered racism in the North.
The Ku Klux Klan, motivated by fear of racial diversity and equality,
flourished in western New York. Even well-intentioned white people
couldn't escape the bondage of unconscious racism. This often led to
awkward incidents, such as a supper Thurman spent with a family
after he spoke at a local congregation's men's club. He struck up a
close relationship with the family's five-year-old daughter at the dinner table. During the meal, the family cat made himself a nuisance
and elicited the child's repeated rebuke, "Stop, nigger, stop!" Thur-

man recalls, "At that moment I realized with a start that family was unaware of the implications of the incident."[23] This is a reminder to all of us who come from privilege that it is essential for us to "watch our language" as we prayerfully and mindfully examine the benefits of the privilege that comes from race, economics, gender, or sexuality and our own implicit social and legal "superiority."

In the years ahead, Thurman rose to prominence as a faculty member at Morehouse; Dean of Chapel at Howard University; pastor of America's first intentionally multi-racial congregation, the Church of the Fellowship of All Peoples; and ultimately the first African American Dean of Chapel at a primarily white university, Boston University. In each case, Thurman felt called to leave significant and stable positions to follow God's vision. Well established at Howard University, where he had created unique programs in spiritual formation and contemplative worship, Thurman initially balked when he felt the call to help found the Church of the Fellowship of All Peoples in San Francisco, California. As Thurman recalls, he received guidance when "a motto used by the British War Resisters League flooded my mind: 'It is madness to sail a sea that has never been sailed before, to look for a land, the existence of which is a question. If Columbus had reflected thus, he never would have weighed anchor, but with this madness he discovered a new world.'"[24]

Thurman joined with a white Presbyterian minister to embrace the uncertain future and together they created a multi-racial congregation, reaching out to artists, intellectuals, spiritual seekers, and working people with innovative programs to join body, mind, and spirit through the use of the arts, poetry, dance, and spiritual practices. Firmly established at the Church of the Fellowship of All Peoples, Thurman once more was called to a new adventure. Like Abraham and Sarah, Howard and Sue Thurman left the familiar to return to the

East Coast, where Thurman accepted the position of Dean of Marsh Chapel at Boston University and Professor of Spiritual Disciplines and Resources at the Graduate School of Theology. Despite the opportunities that came with the new appointment, the journey was painful. It involved leaving beloved friends and an innovative program. But, when we recognize that God is with us in our travels, our lives become a holy adventure in which we share in God's dream for us and the world. At Boston University Thurman continued joining the intellectual and spiritual aspects of life by providing spiritual exercises and meditation practices in addition to sermons, prayers, and hymns.

Thurman made his great spiritual insights available far beyond his academic milieu. A prolific devotional writer and popular speaker, Thurman was described by a major magazine as one of America's most influential preachers. Tragically, achieving recognition and renown rarely shields a person of color from prejudice and disrespect. Even with his prominence, Thurman could not escape the impact of racism. On a train trip from Chicago to Memphis, Thurman sat across from an elderly white lady, who took umbrage at his presence. "What is *that* doing in this car?" she complained to the conductor as he was taking tickets. To which the conductor responded, "*That* has a ticket." Over the next fifty miles, as the woman complained, Thurman felt a growing resentment to his presence in the railroad car.[25] Thurman would later write that as he struggled to deal with these situations, he discovered that God was with him through his trials, providing him with strength and wisdom. Thurman learned that soul force, born of a commitment to "center down" to experience the Holy Spirit's "sighs too deep for words" through prayer and meditation, was the primary antidote to feelings of worthlessness and hatred. He modeled and taught this lesson to others, such as Martin Luther King, Jr., helping them spiritually prepare for the trials they would face.

Looking back on his professional and spiritual life, Howard also recognized God's presence in unexpected encounters that challenged him to rethink his faith. As a result of his growing reputation as a spiritual teacher and crusader for peace, Thurman and his wife, Sue, were invited to meet with Christian and non-Christian social activists across the globe. Pivotal to Thurman's spiritual journey was a pilgrimage that he and Sue took to India in 1935 as part of a delegation of African American Christians. In India, he was confronted by an Indian social activist who challenged Thurman's commitment to Jesus: How can you be a Christian and African American, given the reality of Christian slave ownership, Christian use of the church and the Bible to justify slavery and Jim Crow, and ongoing racism among Christians? Thurman recognized the sincerity and truth of the question and responded:

> I make a careful distinction between Christianity
> and the religion of Jesus. My judgment about
> slavery and racial prejudice relative to Christianity
> is far more devastating than yours could ever be.
> From my investigation and study, the religion of
> Jesus projected a creative solution to the pressing
> problem of survival for the minority of which He
> was a part in the Greco-Roman world.[26]

Throughout his life, Thurman asserted that Jesus was on the side of the dispossessed and marginalized. The spirit of Jesus inspires those in every generation who seek "freedom, liberty, and justice, for all people, black, white, red, yellow, saint, sinner, rich or poor."[27] Though he seldom participated in sit-ins and marches, Thurman inspired and gave spiritual counsel to activists such as Martin Luther King, Jr., who carried Thurman's *Jesus and the Disinherited* in his satchel during the height of the civil rights movement.

During their Indian adventure, Howard and Sue Thurman had an opportunity to meet and engage in conversation with Mahatma Gandhi, who asked them to sing "Were You There When They Crucified My Lord?" Gandhi then noted "I feel that this song gets to the entire root of the experience of the human race under the spread of the healing wings of suffering."[28] We are all bound in a solidarity of those who experience suffering, whether through racism, sexism, homophobia, poverty, age, marginalization, or illness. In recognizing that the "least of these," can apply to any of us, by the choice of others or the accidents of faith, we can cultivate spacious spirits that transform suffering into hope and fear into love.

Thurman saw divine providence guiding his steps, ever inviting him toward new horizons and uncharted territories. After retiring from Boston University, Thurman returned to San Francisco, where he established the Howard Thurman Educational Trust, dedicated to supporting African American college students, both intellectually and spiritually, especially in the Deep South. Thurman's holy adventure from "Jim Crow" Daytona Beach to global acclaim reflected his understanding of God's gentle providence present in the positive as well as negative events of our lives. God is at work in our cells and souls, our hearts and minds, and despite the challenges we face and the machinations of those who try to keep us down, God guides our pilgrimage toward the far horizons of faithfulness and freedom.

We are children of divine providence. When we awaken to God's wisdom and commit ourselves to God's way, we discover pathways beyond our wildest dreams. Looking back on his life, Thurman notes:

> God was everywhere and utterly identified with
> every single thing, incident or person. The phrases

"the God of Abraham, Isaac, or Jacob," or again, "the God of Jesus" were continuously luminous to me in my journey . . . . The older I have grown, the more it is clear that what I needed to hold me to my path was the sure knowledge that I was committed to a single journey with but a single goal—a way toward life. In formal and religious terms this meant for me the disclosure of the Will of God.[29]

A PRACTICE FOR PROPHETIC HEALING

Howard Thurman speaks of his life—and ours—as a holy adventure in which God reveals divine wisdom and provides divine energy and guidance to explore new possibilities of faithfulness. Divine providence guides our steps. Neither coercive or determinative, divine providence awaits our decisions, provides pathways in challenging times, and awakens us to new possibilities grounded in the interplay of divine call and human response.

Looking at your life, where have you experienced God's providential care and guidance? Take some time to reflect on significant moments in your life. Can you identify moments when God provided a path to the future or new insights and inspirations where you had only seen a dead end? Right now, at this point in your life, where is God guiding you? Recognizing that life is a holy adventure, prayerfully open to God's guidance and energy that can give us more than we could ever ask for or imagine.

Thurman's adventure occurred in the context of racist policies and behaviors, born of America's "original sin" of slavery. The impact of slavery lives on in powerlessness and poverty, voter suppression, and the current rise of white nationalism. Our spiritual journeys in their concreteness occur in the context of America's racist legacy. Accordingly, the second exercise is primarily for people who are of privilege in their social order, and I am one! Perhaps, you are, too. Our sense of unity challenges us to consider our own unique experiences, rising from the positive accidents of our births. The question of white or any other kind of privilege, such as economics, giftedness, or physical health, is not intended to produce guilt but invite transformation and affirmation. We have much to affirm in our ethnicity and families of origin, but if we are white in North America, we often take for granted what many people of color have to fight for daily, and we live our lives with a sense of our worth and equality, while they face ongoing, systemic biases that seek to limit them at every turn.

Often we are unaware of our social and racial privilege. We take for granted that everyone is treated as we are and has the same attitude toward institutions, such as law enforcement and the justice system, as we do. Several years ago I was walking through my neighborhood with a Latino colleague. He was a Brooks Brothers, nattily dressed, dignified academic success. A police car drove by, and the appearance of the local gendarme led us to a conversation about our attitudes toward the police. I noted that now, as a slightly overweight white male, of a certain age (then in my fifties), I was a patrolman's dream and that I no longer feared the police, unlike my hippie days when I was regularly harassed by the "cops." I was surprised when he responded that despite his education, success, and achievements, he still felt anxious whenever a police car drove by.

In prayerfully reflecting on the reality of privilege—if you come from a racially, economically, or socially privileged group—devote a week to being mindful of your life situation: examine what you take for granted that others can only dream of, what social and economic benefits you inherited through no effort of your own, what respect in the community or in the legal system you assume. In your prayerful reflections, imaginatively put yourself in the place of a person of color, a Muslim woman wearing a *hijab*, an undocumented worker, or a person pulled over by the police for "driving while black." Let these contrasting images call you to prayer and to justice-seeking in your community. Ask God to open your eyes and enlarge your spirit toward true holy inclusion.

You may be inspired to read a text such as Julie Landsman's *Growing Up White: A Veteran Teacher Reflects on Racism*, Ibram X. Kendi's *How to Be an Anti-Racist*, Jennifer Harvey's *Raising White Kids*, or Bryan Stevenson's *Just Mercy*, which has also been made into a film, to expand your awareness of white privilege and begin to heal your racial assumptions. On your own holy adventure with God as companion, in what ways do your new insights guide you toward contemplative activism on behalf of the marginalized, oppressed, and disenfranchised?

CHAPTER FIVE

MYSTICISM
AND SOCIAL ACTION

*I have sought a way of life that could come
under the influence of, and be informed by,
the fruits of the inner life. The cruel vicissitudes
of the social situation in which I have been
forced to live in American society have made it
vital for me to seek resources, or a resource to which
I could have access as I sought means for sustaining
the personal enterprise of my life beyond
all the ravages inflicted upon it by the brutalities
of the social order.*[30]

Howard Thurman's lectures on "Mysticism and Social Action,"
delivered at First Unitarian Church in Berkeley, California, on Oc-
tober 13 and 14, 1978, reveal Thurman's lifelong quest to join spirituality and social transformation. Given just a few years before his
death, these lectures are a poetic harvest of over forty years of theological reflection and spiritual practice. In words that anticipate the
political and social polarization of the twenty-first century, Thurman
describes the personal and social context of his lectures. On the one
hand, Thurman's spiritual meditations come from one who is "an

outsider in the community of power, where most of the life and death decisions are made which control the common life," and who must struggle daily to affirm his identity and find his place in a society whose structures often disregard his voice and value.[31] Living in an implicitly, if not explicitly, racist social and political environment, Thurman asserts that "it has been vital for me to find within myself the door that no man could shut, to locate resources that are uniquely mine, to which I must be true if the personal enterprise of my life is to be sustained despite the ravages inflicted upon it by society."[32]

Thurman believed that his only hope to find wholeness, self-esteem, and love for those who looked down upon him as an inferior was to cultivate his inner life through prayer and meditation. Moreover, in the self-esteem that emerged from experiencing God's presence in his life and the world, Thurman found that he was able to protest injustice without polarizing or demonizing those who sought to oppress him, and to speak God's prophetic word in hope that those in power could awaken to the better angels of their nature. Speaker of the House Tip O'Neill once asserted that all politics is local. The same can be said for spirituality. Though we may ascend to the heavens, the "ladder of angels," as Jacob discovers at Beth-El, is planted first here on earth (Genesis 28:10-22). The gateway to God, Beth-El, as Jacob discerns, is found in the context of the complexities of history, politics, and our inner life and personal behavior. Thurman's deep commitment to spiritual transformation enabled him to experience personal wholeness in a society that often denied his identity and dignity as a child of God. In words from one of the anchor passages in this book, I believe that Thurman's personal path enabled him "to be strong enough to carry the heavy stones of the spirit which are necessary for the foundations of the kingdom of friendly men underneath a friendly sky."[33]

Thurman recognizes that his reflections are rooted in his experiences of the chaos, racism, violence, and depersonalization of the current social order, in which kindness and empathy in social and political relationships have become increasingly rare. In words that could easily describe the political and social divisions of our time, Thurman notes, "Here, I am referring to the widespread disintegration of the mood of tenderness, which makes us falter, hesitate, or become immobile in efforts to understand and to like each other."[34] In the twenty-first century, insults and bullying come from the highest echelons of American politics. The once-friendly Facebook, in its inception characterized primarily by witty quotes and photos of family, meals, and holiday spots, has become a platform for hate speech, false news reports, personal insult, cyberbullying, and divisive bots from antagonistic political and national groups.

In such a contrary environment, we need holistic forms of mysticism embodied by mystic activists: not otherworldly mystics, but spiritual leaders who are both heavenly minded, with eyes on the prize of everlasting life, and earthly engaged, seeking God's realm "on earth as it is in heaven." This holistic spirituality embodies what the Quaker scholar Rufus Jones described as "affirmative mysticism." For Thurman, mysticism is prophetic and joins contemplation and action, and the inner and outer journeys. As Thurman notes, "For our purposes, then, mysticism is defined as the response of the individual to a personal encounter with God within his own soul. This is my working definition. Such a response is total, effecting the inner quality of the life and its outward expression."[35]

Having experienced God's presence in the depths of her own soul, the mystic glimpses the signs of God's presence in all humankind, including those who perpetrate injustice or manipulate the political system for personal or economic gain. In the solitude of mystical experience, the spiritual pilgrim feels the deep and concrete interconnectedness of life. All creation is joined in one great pulse of divine energy. The detachment and solitude that characterize mystical experience leads to self-transcendence and the expansion of self-interest to include the well-being of the community and the planet. Mystics, in the spirit of Jesus, grow in wisdom and stature (Luke 2:52). They see our common humanity, empathize with the suffering of the oppressed, and embrace contrasting viewpoints, even viewpoints they continue to oppose, and in the process begin to move from polarization to reconciliation in personal relationships and political involvement.

Detachment from individual self-interest inspires actions that promote the well-being of the mystic's human siblings and all creation. Having experienced God as the source of all creation, the mystic desires that all people experience this same sense of wholeness, according to their unique personalities, cultures, and life-experiences. When mystics observe conditions that threaten a person's encounter with God, they feel compelled to confront them. Injustice of all kinds stifles the imagination, dampens dreams, traumatizes spirits, and forces people to focus on mere survival rather than spiritual fulfillment. The mystic shares philosopher Alfred North Whitehead's belief that the goal of life is, first, simply to live, then to live well, and ultimately to live better, recognizing that these are spiritual as well as material categories.[36] Jesus' ministerial vision, "I came that they may have life, and have it abundantly" (John 10:10) applies as much to social conditions that undergird personal well-being as to spiritual commitments. "Social action, therefore, is an expression of resistance against whatever tends to, or separates one, from the experience of God, who is the ground of his being."[37]

The mystic understands that healthy societies provide an essential foundation for experiences of spiritual wholeness. Improving the social, political, and economic order opens the door for the leisure and dignity necessary for intellectual, aesthetic, and spiritual growth. In contrast, when people do not have adequate food, housing, security, social equality, and legal protection, they seldom pursue intellectual and spiritual growth. Trauma haunts their daily lives and mistrust feeds their spirits. The mystic's social agenda ultimately "has to do with the removal of all that prevents God from coming to himself in the life of the individual. Whatever there is that blocks this, calls for action."[38]

While there are many pathways of political involvement, social action is a necessity for those whose experiences of God have led them to discover God's movements in all creation. "For the mystic, social action is sacramental, because it is not an end in itself. Always, it is the individual who must be addressed, located and released, underneath his misery and his hunger and his destitution. That whatever may be blocking his way to his own center where his altar may be found, this must be removed."[39] The mystic realizes that the rich and the poor, the oppressor and the oppressed, may be equally alienated from their deepest selves, despite their economic and social differences. The soul-destroying nature of poverty and injustice is obvious and must be addressed immediately with wise personal and political action. The powerful and wealthy perpetrators of injustice are also in spiritual jeopardy. With all their advantages and privilege, they have turned their gaze from beauty of the heavens and human life to the banality of oppression and manipulation. One can gain the world, as Jesus says, and lose one's soul, caught up in consumerism, power, entitlement, and self-gratification. The oppressor's injustice ultimately stunts their own soul. The hate, evident in the behaviors of those who threaten violence toward those who differ from them racially or politically, betrays deep insecurity, fear, and mistrust in the fundamental holiness of life. Political leaders who spew hate and promote chaos and alienation are to be pitied as well as opposed. Bravado and boasting often hides anxiety, insecurity, and envy. Purveyors of racial division often sacrifice their souls and intimate relationships for short-term political gain.

Social change can be painful for those who have perpetuated injustice. They must see the negative impact of their actions on those who suffer as a result of their conscious and/or unconscious, though often intended, racism, sexism, and materialism. In Thurman's language, they may need to be "shocked" out of their complacency, sense of entitlement, and assumptions of privilege and superiority. The goal of experiences of "shock" through protest, picketing, and boycotts is to awaken those who perpetrate injustice to their connection with those whom they knowingly or unknowingly harm. The goal of political challenge is to agitate the comfortable and awaken them to their deeper humanity as well as the humanity of those who are harmed by their actions or apathy. In Thurman's words:

> What is important for the mystic is that the purpose
> of the shock treatment is to hold before the offender
> a mirror that registers an image of himself, that
> reflects the image of those who suffer at his hands.
> The total function of such action is to tear men from
> any alignments that prevent them from putting
> themselves in the other person's place, but it must
> never be forgotten that the central concern of the
> mystic is to seek to remove anything that prevents
> the individual from free and easy access to his own
> altar-stair that is in his own heart.[40]

In being shocked out of complacency and privilege—and sometimes intentional injustice—the oppressor is given the opportunity to reclaim her or his own soul and discover her or his solidarity with all creation in God's beloved community. The healing of the oppressor becomes a catalyst for the embodiment of God's vision of Shalom in daily interactions and political and business decision-making.

Even if the mystic herself must suffer for the cause of justice, "a way has to be found to restore and discover self-worth, authentic identity, the chief manifestation of which is a consciousness of the in-dwelling presence of which the mystic speaks."[41] In this way, the mystic achieves her or his spiritual goal, that all may experience holiness and, in so doing, God will be "all in all" (I Corinthians 15:28).

A PRACTICE FOR
PROPHETIC HEALING

Mystical experiences cannot be forced. They come often intuitively or unexpectedly, even when we are going in the wrong direction, as was the case of the Apostle Paul's Damascus Road experience (Acts 9:1–9). Yet mystical experiences can be prepared for, loosely and without demanding a particular result. There are many gifts in the body of Christ and we cannot dictate in advance our unique spiritual gifts (I Corinthians 12:1–13). In the spirit of Howard Thurman, I define mysticism as any encounter with God that awakens us to the holiness of ourselves and others, that opens us to a God-filled universe, and then deepens our sense of solidarity with the human and non-human worlds. Mystics revise Jacob's exclamation, following his dream of a ladder of angels ascending from earth to heaven and back again, with the affirmation, "God was in this place—and now I know it!"

In this practice of prophetic healing, place yourself simply in God's presence. There is something of God in each of us—something of God in you—and in all creation, including those who use their wealth and power to perpetuate injustice and ecological destruction. Trusting the divine pulse moving through all creation, read meditatively parts of Psalms 148 and 150:

Praise the LORD!
Praise the LORD from the heavens;
praise God in the heights!
Praise God, all angels;
praise God, all heavenly host!
Praise God, sun and moon;
praise God, all you shining stars!
Praise God, you highest heavens,
and you waters above the heavens!
Praise the LORD from the earth,
you sea monsters and all deeps,
fire and hail, snow and frost,
stormy wind fulfilling his command!
Mountains and all hills,
fruit trees and all cedars!
Wild animals and all cattle,
creeping things and flying birds!
Kings of the earth and all peoples,
princes and all rulers of the earth!
Young men and women alike,
old and young together!
Let everything that breathes praise God!
Praise God!
(Psalm 148:1-4, 7-11; Psalm 150:6, author paraphrase)

In response to the psalm, open to a pulse of praise flowing through you, uniting you with all creation, human and non-human. Feel one great breath filling you with life and taking you from separation to unity. In this symphony of praise, see if you can experience a connection with those you have perceived as "other." Visualize something of God in a politician whose actions and character alienate you. Visualize something of God's presence in someone who challenges your assumptions about certain political or racial issues, without trying to discern the accuracy of their critique. (Later, you may choose to explore your own limitations as well as the limitations, or inaccuracies, of their position.) Experience your unity with the flora and fauna, the fish of the sea, the humpbacked whale, the plankton, the air. See your face mirrored in the face of people experiencing homelessness, refugee status, and opioid addiction.

This exercise may involve praying with your eyes open or while watching cable television news. Any practice can be holy if we enter with a desire to experience God's still, small voice in ourselves and those we encounter. Conclude this practice asking God for one tangible way you can bring greater unity to your community and the political order. Listen for divine guidance in your intuitions, dreams, inclinations, the news, and your apparently "chance" encounters.

CHAPTER SIX
LIBERATING MYSTICISM

As prophets of the most High God,
it is your divine assignment to announce that man
lives his days under the persistent scrutiny of God:
that God is at stake in man's day.
You must live and proclaim a faith that will
make men affirm themselves and their fellowmen
as children of God. You must lay your lives
on the altar of social change so that wherever
you are the Kingdom of God is at hand.[42]

At the heart of the mystic's experience is the desire to free oneself and others from spiritual bondage. While some see spiritual liberation as other-worldly, Thurman proclaims that the mystical unity he felt as a child inspired him to experience the holiness of life and the interdependence of creation. The Divine Spirit who energetically moves through all creation, bringing forth a world of wondrous diversity, seeks to be known by every creature, according to its unique gifts. Though global in impact, the Divine Spirit is intimately related to every creature in an ongoing process of call and response. The psalmist proclaims "let everything that breathes praise God," and this includes the non-human as well as human world (Psalm 150:6). The Gospel of Thomas proclaims, "Cleave the wood and I am there" (Passage 77).

Jesus asserted that the Spirit of God inspired his mission to heal the sick, release the captives, and set the oppressed free (Luke 4:18). The Apostle Paul proclaimed, "For freedom Christ has set us free. Stand firm, therefore, and do not submit again to a yoke of slavery" (Galatians 5:1). While the words of Jesus and Paul have been interpreted as purely spiritual and thus unrelated to the historical realities of politics and economics, both Paul and Jesus were rooted in the holistic spirituality of the Hebraic prophets, who asserted that God feels the pain of those who suffer from economic and social injustice. Inspired by their own intimate encounters with the living God, the prophets saw social injustice as a denial of God's sovereignty over all things and compassion for all people. The prophetic witness of the Hebraic scriptures describes God as concerned with integrity in weights and measures and business practices, mortgages, and economic distribution.

Salvation, or wholeness, can never be separated from the social conditions within which people live. Injustice, racism, and poverty are sins against our loving Creator as well as God's creatures and may, as Amos proclaims, lead to a famine on hearing the word of God among those who oppress the poor (Amos 8:11). God disregards our temples, doctrines, and rituals when we turn our backs on God's call to "let justice roll down like waters, and righteousness like an ever-flowing stream" (Amos 5:24).

Following the Hebraic prophets, Thurman believed that mystical experiences lead to social action on behalf of the dispossessed and downtrodden. The mystic challenges everything that stands in the way of people experiencing their full potential as God's beloved children. While the mystic may choose voluntary poverty and martyrdom, he or she also is profoundly aware that when people are forced to live in poverty, endure institutional violence, and are denied basic human rights, their spirits are stunted and their hearts broken. We need to seek "a friendly world of friendly people," undergirded by a friendly social order, Thurman averred.

Prophetic mysticism has as its goal liberation from unhealthy and imprisoning spiritual attachments. It also seeks to liberate people from the chains of servitude, exclusion, and racism that imprison the body and spirit alike. Much to the surprise of the powerful, prophetic liberation also seeks to free the oppressor from her or his attachment to consumption, power, and violence. Bound together in an intricate fabric of destiny, the rich and poor and oppressor and oppressed find freedom together in communities of healing and partnership.

Thurman's role as one of the first African American liberation theologians has been neglected by many commentators on the civil rights movement. Yet Thurman's spirituality of compassionate and inclusive justice-seeking influenced many of the leaders of the civil rights movement, including Martin Luther King, Jr.

First published in 1949, *Jesus and the Disinherited* is both personal and professional in nature. Thurman writes as an academic, spiritual leader, and pastor, but his writing is also the reflection of an African American living daily in a society that challenges his dignity despite his people's numerous contributions to all aspects of American life and freedom. The text is written to respond to those "who stand with their backs against the wall" and who are often neglected by a church that has sided with the powerful and wealthy to the detriment of people experiencing poverty and injustice.[43] Then and now, the church must decide what it will say to the poor, dispossessed, and disinherited.

Thurman believes that it is important to encounter the real Jesus of history and not a figment of the imagination created by Euro-American maintainers of the economic and racial status quo. The historical Jesus was a lower middle-class Jew, a member of a minority group, living in a state of constant oppression, unable to determine his personal agenda and subject without dealing with the indignities that characterize institutional oppression. Thurman notes that "there was no moment in all his years when he was free."[44] Far from being other-worldly, the way of Jesus was profoundly historical as it addressed spiritual, physical, social, and economic survival in an inherently unjust society. Thurman notes the "striking similarity between the social position of Jesus in Palestine and that of the vast majority of American Negroes."[45] Tragically, the injustices Jesus faced in the first century are still experienced in today's Palestine, in the streets of urban America, on the USA borderlands, in the ongoing oppression of women around the world, and widespread governmental policies that favor the rich at the expense of the poor and disenfranchised.

Thurman notes the spiritual damage that injustice creates among the socially and politically disenfranchised. On the one hand, the world's dispossessed people can easily succumb to fear, hatred, and dishonesty. They often begin to accept the judgments of the oppressor as legitimate, especially the judgment that they are inferior, incompetent, and unable to manage their own affairs. There is, as Thurman laments, "but a step from being despised to despising oneself."[46] On the other hand, oppression stunts the imaginations and dreams of people of all ages, especially children. Survival needs trump creativity and playful abandon in children in the Sudan, Syrian refugee camps, inner city ghettos, and Appalachian hollers. Liberation begins first with a new vision of life, profoundly different from that of the persecutor. Whereas oppressors deny the dignity of the poor and disenfranchised, judging them as moral, spiritual, and intellectual inferiors, "the core of the analysis of Jesus is that man is a child of God, the God of life that sustains all of nature and guarantees all the intricacies of life-process itself."[47] God numbers the hairs on our heads, cares for the affairs of our lives, and has a stake in each person's spiritual well-being and fulfillment. God's love for all creation challenges us to affirm the dignity, equality, and common humanity of black and white, rich and poor, male and female, gay and straight, cisgender and transgender, and oppressor and oppressed. Only when we see all people as God's beloved children can we honor each other, despite our differences, and find common ground in creating a healthy and just society.

Thurman asserts that the "religion of Jesus makes the love-ethic central" and challenges us to see the image of God in those whom we presume to be our enemies.[48] To embody this life-transforming spirit today, the privileged and underprivileged both need transformed hearts and minds to jointly work for the creation of a "common environment for the purpose of normal experiences of fellowship," the first step of which is "a common sharing of a sense of mutual worth and value."[49] This must occur in concrete experiences that are natural and free and can be found in the experience of praying and talking with one another. In such encounters, self-transcendence and sacrifice are possible for those who were formerly oppressor and oppressed. Experiences of empathy replace feelings of alienation when we realize our common unity as God's beloved children. The Apostle Paul's quest for unity in the Christian community becomes the norm for society in all its wondrous diversity: "There is no longer Jew or Greek, there is no longer slave or free, there is no longer male and female; for all of you are one in Christ Jesus" (Galatians 3:28).

In a community characterized by justice-seeking, otherness and contrast become the basis for creative personal and social transformation. Our personal freedom is blended with our responsibility to affirm the dignity of those around us. Recognizing that we can all be imprisoned by our beliefs, ethnicities, and social standing, the Apostle Paul proclaims that authentic liberation comes from loving identification with God's way rather than our own limited interests and prejudices. This may involve sacrifice and it may also involve asserting your dignity in oppressive situations:

> "It is for freedom that Christ has set us free. Stand firm, then, and do not let yourselves be burdened again by a yoke of slavery" (Galatians 5:1). Our freedom to change our attitudes is the intersection of mysticism and liberation. Each one of us can claim a role in bringing healing to our families, neighborhoods, and nation. It is urgent to hold steadily in the mind the utter responsibility of the solitary individual to do everything with all his heart and mind to arrest the development of the consequences of private and personal evil resulting from the interaction of the impersonal forces that surround us. To cancel out between you and another all personal and private evil, to place your life squarely on the side of the good thing because it is good, and for no other reason, is to anticipate the Kingdom of God at the level of your functioning.[50]

Thurman believes that we can humbly transcend our personal limitations and the walls erected between ourselves and others to find a common spiritual identity and purposes that unite us in heal-

ing the social order. In this liberating moment, regardless of our no-
toriety or influence in the larger society (or lack thereof), we can be
forerunners of God's realm of Shalom, bringing healing to the earth
one encounter at a time.

A PRACTICE FOR PROPHETIC HEALING

Commitment to liberation is both individual and corporate, inner and outer. It may involve sacrifice as well as protest, and it is a moment by moment process of surrendering our agenda to a larger, more holistic vision. For example, this morning as I was writing, my oldest grandson woke up and asked me to play a game with him. I wanted to continue my writing, as I felt I was on a writer's roll. I responded, "Give me a minute to finish this paragraph, and I'm all yours." We had a great time together. An hour later, I said, "How about we both take fifteen minutes on our own, and then read together after that?" He agreed, and we both finished our appointed projects. While my example of an adult-child relationship may seem insignificant compared to issues of corporate and political injustice, it is a microcosm of the sacrificial living necessary for national and planetary and personal survival. People of privilege are challenged to risk downward mobility, share the reins of power, and recognize that survival trumps personal self-interest. Liberation means, from the point of view of the privileged, sacrificing our time, talent, and treasures so others can enjoy economic justice and access to power.

Liberation also involves social involvement. In the spirit of Thurman's contemplative vision, pause to "center down" in silence with the attention of listening for God's call to social involvement in your community and nation, regardless of its personal inconvenience. We are called to be "peaceful warriors," working hard and persistently to bring justice into the world, while honoring our own and others' identities as God's beloved children, regardless of our initial attitudes toward them. In the silence, listen for God's voice amid the many conflicting voices in your mind. Awaken to the wisdom of deep silence, and then in response, make a commitment to become involved in a local as well as global initiative, such as Grandmothers Against Gun Violence, Bread for the World, Amnesty International, the Poor People's March, the Southern Christian Leadership Conference, the Southern Poverty Law Center, or a phone call on a pressing issue to your local county, state, or national representative. You can't do everything, but you can do what God places before you as your calling in healing the world.

CHAPTER SEVEN

FINDING COMMON GROUND

The place where imagination shows
its greatest power as the agent of God is in the
miracle which it creates, when one man, standing
where he is, is able, while remaining there,
to put himself in another man's place.[51]

Thurman believed that social transformation joins theology and spirituality and invites us to transcend our particular perspectives to empathize more fully with others' experiences. Whether we are active in a religious community or consider ourselves spiritual but not religious, agnostic, or atheist, we all see the world through certain lenses that provide the foundation for what we notice, value, and affirm. Our lenses provide us with important and valuable insights, but they also limit our perspectives. I see the world through a variety of lenses, including some I have inherited and others I have achieved: my identity as a European American, my family of origin as middle class with a focus on education, my well-read parents, my boomer life experience, my Ph.D. and academic and pastoral career, my access to political and economic opportunities, my identity as a heterosexual male. These are all valuable, important, and good, provided that they do not exclude or diminish the experience and insights of those with other lenses.

The inclusive spiritual vision Thurman sought opens us to more deeply understand the experiences of those who differ from us, politically, economically, racially, and religiously. In the spirit of William Blake, there are moments when the "doors of perception" are cleansed and we experience a broader, more diverse world of countless viewpoints and life experiences. These experiences of suddenly perceiving more clearly, whether dramatic or mundane, may challenge the current ways we see the world and awaken us to new levels of reality. To paraphrase the Apostle Paul, in such moments, we are no longer conformed to the world of our religion, social location, or ethnicity, but are transformed by God's renewing our mind (Romans 12:2).

Initially blinded by the light of Christ while traveling to persecute Jesus' first followers, the Apostle Paul, once certain of his religious orthodoxy, discovers the reality of God in Christ, joining all people in a dynamic and interdependent community, the body of Christ. His narrowly orthodox Jewish theology and ethics collapses as a result of his Damascus Road encounter with Christ and he becomes the champion of the new religious movement in which everyone had a role in the body of Christ, in which "there is no longer Jew or Greek, there is no longer slave or free, there is no longer male and female; for all of you are one in Christ Jesus" (Galatians 3:28). Paul's mystical encounter with the Risen Christ led him to create a new community that overcame social, economic, ethnic, and religious isolation. Paul discovered that despite their ethnic and historical differences, the Jews and Gentiles of this nascent new religion could find common ground and community in their relationship with Jesus Christ.

Paul's Letter to the Galatians is a sustained affirmation that there are no second-class Christians. Separate but equal not only can destroy a nation; it also can threaten the survival of an emerging spiritual movement. This is the ethical point of Paul's Letters to the Galatians and Philemon. Seeing our unity in Christ with those serving as slaves, we soon realize that slavery must be abolished—first, among Christians and then in the larger society. Recognizing that ethnic diversity, such as communities of Jews and Gentiles worshiping with one another in the early church, deepens and enriches rather than divides, inspires us to treasure the spiritual gifts of many cultures.

Today, we need to realize that we are standing together on holy ground. The social order is both polarized and fragmented. Liberals and conservatives seldom share in creative dialogue. They listen to their own boutique internet news feeds and cable news broadcasts, which for the most part are aimed at encouraging divisiveness and controversy rather than promoting unity. In the religious world, one group claims that it possesses the fullness of the gospel, while another group denounces that same group's legitimacy in order to bolster its own self-affirmation. The Christian vision of the "body of Christ," in which "if one member suffers, all suffer together with it; if one member is honored, all rejoice together with it" (1 Corinthians 12:26) is eclipsed by "me, first," "nation, first," and "denomination, first." The mosaic, affirmed in the Great Seal of the United States of America, *E pluribus unum*, "out of many one" has been defaced by the idolatries of ideology, economics, race, and orthodoxy that threaten our nation's survival.

Perhaps the dream of common ground has always been a hope rather than a reality. Still, we need to get out of our gated political worlds and allow God to renew our minds, opening us to broader horizons of human experience and unity within God's wondrous diversity of human and non-human life.

The reality of divisiveness is as old as the biblical legend of the Tower of Babel. But, with the immediacy of the 24/7 news cycle and internet feeds, not to mention the proliferation of fake news intended to create social and political division, the need for common ground becomes more crucial than ever before. Our communities, congregations, country, and planet cannot survive the fragmented world views that are sweeping our nation and defining our foreign policy. Isolated, individualistic, and siloed visions of reality will eventually undermine both our nation and the planet. The rugged individualist is going against the nature of reality as well as her or his own self-interest, since no person or nation is an island able to survive without the support of others. Though we must affirm our uniqueness, reflected in our own inner lives and ethnic backgrounds, no person or nation can "separate himself from his fellows, for mutual interdependence is the characteristic of all life."[52]

Thurman's lifetime search for community culminated in the publication in 1971 of *The Search for Common Ground*. In his seventh decade, Thurman looks back at a lifetime of searching for spiritually grounded options for peacemakers and justice seekers. Though, like many of Thurman's books, *The Search for Common Ground* ascends into the heavens of theological and philosophical reflection, his quest is highly personal, concrete, and political in nature. Like the Gentiles Paul describes in the Letter to the Galatians, Thurman writes as an outsider, who is asked to regularly prove his worth and adapt to the majority culture to receive a hearing in the legal and intellectual communities. Thurman cannot escape the color of his skin and the five-hundred-year impact of America's "original sin," slavery and its destruction of African American culture and family. Even as a learned scholar, with a national reputation, he must, at times, face the reality that many European Americans whose education, intellect, and accomplishments are greatly inferior to his own claim unmerited racial superiority in relationship to Thurman and people of color despite their achievements.

Despite his irenic spirit, there is no idealistic singing of "Kum Ba Yah" around Thurman's theological campfire. His spirituality is quietly prophetic and passionately transformative. He recognizes the realities of racism and injustice. But these realities do not daunt Thurman; he still quests for the equality essential to realizing our hope of common ground in a pluralistic society—and he invites us to join him in this inspired and inspiring pursuit.

The quest for common ground is an "impossible possibility." But, for Thurman, holding on to what appear to be paradoxes can save us. Thurman offers no panacea in our quest for common ground. Finding common ground with those who hold contrasting political and social perspectives will be hard work, especially in our highly charged cultural and political environment. Although Thurman does not explicitly say so, his writings suggest that the quest for unity in diversity is not only theological, spiritual, and political; it also relies on a commitment to truth and to a quest to separate fact from falsehood. Although no one individual's perspective can encompass the whole, we need to begin the journey toward unity in diversity with Daniel Patrick Moynihan's maxim: "You're entitled to your own opinions. You're not entitled to your own facts." While everyone on occasion may be misinformed, we need to make a commitment to discerning the "facts at hand" in any situation, whether it relates to economics, climate change, prison populations, or congregational finances. It means making an ethical commitment to radical honesty in a world in which politicians glibly violate the ninth commandment, "you shall not bear false witness against your neighbor," with every speech and news conference.

The first step in the quest for common ground requires us to speak simply and honestly, giving those with whom we disagree the benefit of accurately reporting their positions and recognizing both their failures and their achievements. We need to move from language of opposition to language of contrast, listening before we critique and looking for the best in others' viewpoints while recognizing the fallibility of our own political and faith perspectives.

Second, Thurman believes, it is essential to recognize that "all men belong to each other, and he who shuts himself away diminishes himself, and he who shuts another away from him destroys himself."[53] There is an underlying sense of unity, despite our differences, grounded in our common origins, environment, and destiny. Relationship, not isolated individuality, is at the heart of reality. While the integrity and uniqueness of each person—or plant or animal—must be affirmed, our individual uniqueness and achievement depends on the ambient environment that provides possibility and limitation. Gratitude for the gifts of others liberates our individual and communal gifts and inspires our common imagination and quest for a "more perfect union."

Third, this ultimate interdependence is the gift of divine wisdom and creativity. With process theologians, Thurman sees "God in all things, and all things in God." Thurman believes that God "stands in relation to all existence somewhat as the mind in man stands in relationship to his space-time existence."[54] God is the creative spirit and wise energy present in every creature, giving each creature life and shaping each creature's destiny. God's love inspires the world process, joins diverse communities, and lovingly embraces all creation in God's ongoing relationship with the world. From this perspective, each of us is touched by God. An essential and original holiness joins and inspires us as a result of our diversity.

Fourth, the universality of God's presence and revelation undergirds our awareness of the image of God in each person, including those with whom we differ. We need to recognize that God's image is still being born among us—in one another. God seeks to realize God's dream of Shalom in the historical process and in our own timebound and often-ambiguous lives. There is a creative movement of life, a growing edge, which moves subtly through all creation and every human enterprise. This growing edge of hope will be realized, and the moral arc of history will eventually triumph despite the roadblocks we place in its path. God's movement in history awakens the holy in us, in our relationships with others, and in our quest to go from enmity to community.

Confident that we are God's beloved, touched and shaped by divine artistry, we no longer need to fear contrasting opinions or diverse expressions of humanity. Contrast becomes the foundation of creativity and beauty in the cultural environment. Within the contrasts of life, we can experience God's quest for creative transformation and commit ourselves even in this chaotic time to becoming prophetic healers inspiring common purpose among diverse perspectives.

A PRACTICE FOR PROPHETIC HEALING

Empathy is the foundation of common ground. Empathetic spirituality involves recognizing our commonality as God's children and, then, seeking to experience the uniqueness of the other in her or his wonder and limitation.

Empathy is the gift of paying attention, of prayerfully looking beneath the surface of another's life to awaken to their deeper experience. There is a story of a neighbor observing the sculptor Michelangelo rolling a boulder up a hill and onto his porch. Already curious, he was overwhelmed with curiosity when the sculptor began pounding on the rough-hewn boulder. He crossed the street and asked, "What are you doing, pounding on that boulder?" To which Michelangelo replied, "There's an angel inside and I'm trying to let it out." Beneath the rough rock exterior of a geode is a thing of beauty, beneath the angry surface of your enemy's words and expression is a child of God looking for love. Empathy is the gift of seeing angels hidden in those whose lives and behaviors most challenge us.

Today, make a commitment to nurture feelings of empathy. This involves both vision and action. While this is challenging in our contentious society, we can begin by recognizing that those who differ from us have feelings, too. They too may be anxious, fearful, and worried about the future. Look beneath the newsfeed of the angry white supremacist, the envious and chaotic political leader, the disagreeable church member, or the child having an emotional meltdown to see the holiness within. Pray that your common "better angels" burst forth to bless one another.

Let your vision of common ground guide your thoughts and language, so that your speech be irenic even when you protest, that your protest honors the inner holiness of the other, and that your political disagreements be enlightening to both of you. The quest for empathy may mean listening as well as criticizing. If you encounter someone with whom you have significant political or cultural disagreements and you discern that you can initiate a non-contentious conversation, take time to dialogue rather than dismissing or trying to convince them. Look for areas of common interest that may provide first steps toward seeing the humanity in one another and discovering areas in which you can cooperate in improving your communities.

CHAPTER EIGHT

REVERENCE FOR LIFE

The ante-bellum Negro preacher
was the greatest single factor in determining
the spiritual destiny of the slave community . . . .
When he spoke to his group on an occasional Sabbath
day, he knew what they had lived through during the
weeks; how their total environment had conspired to
din in their minds and spirits the corroding notion that
as human beings they were of no significance.
Thus the one message springing full grown from the
mind of God repeated in many ways a wide range
of variations: "You are not slaves,
you are not 'niggers'; you are God's children." [55]

You are God's children! Regardless what the powerful and wealthy say, I am a child of God and so are you! Reverence for life is at the heart of prophetic healing. The Hebraic prophet Amos mourns over the poor and disposessed, recognizing that their cries are also God's cries. Frustrated and filled with anguish at the experiences of society's marginalized, Amos challenges religious institutions whose apathy and alignment with the powerful and wealthy perpetuates injustices that uproot and destroy families and decimate spirits. We are whole people in which mind, body, spirit, and relationships interpenetrate and shape one another. What damages the body harms the spirit, and what abuses the spirit harms relationships and personal well-being. The oppressor as well as the oppressed is spiritually harmed by injustice.

> Hear this, you that trample on the needy,
> and bring to ruin the poor of the land,
> saying, "When will the new moon be over
> so that we may sell grain;
> and the sabbath,
> so that we may offer wheat for sale?
> We will make the ephah small and the shekel great,
> and practice deceit with false balances,
> buying the poor for silver
> and the needy for a pair of sandals,
> and selling the sweepings of the wheat (Amos 8:4-6).

Amos' prophetic threats—born of his righteous indignation—are a prelude to healing through economic justice. Amos is clear that God was trying to get the Israelites' attention and in the twenty-first century, God wants us to pay attention, too. God wants us to hear the cries of the poor and share in God's empathy with the experiences of the dispossessed. The poor are God's children and deserve respect and fairness. God also seeks the redemption of the wealthy and powerful who, in choosing not to hear God's voice in the cries of the poor, may deaden their senses to hearing God's voice in their own lives. Have your senses gotten too weak to hear God in the cries of others?

Reverence for life is essential to social transformation because in our experiences of reverence, we discover that the cries of the downtrodden echo our own brokenness. There is no "other." No one's experience is alien to our own. The joy of others is our joy, the success of others is our success, the pain and destitution of others is our pain and destitution. Regardless of our social or economic standing, we, too, are "standin' in the need of prayer" and require Divine grace and the support of loving communities to find our way and live God's vision for our lives. God's word to us is "pay attention," then "listen," and then "respond" to suffering wherever it occurs, whether it emerges from accident, disease, natural disaster, or human decision-making. The suffering and forgotten are God's children, too!

Thurman's vision echoes and affirms his older contemporary Albert Schweitzer's image of reverence for life:

> Our love of God is akin to reverent love. God
> is infinite life. Thus the most elementary ethical
> principle, when understood by the heart, means
> that out of reverence for the unfathomable, infinite
> and living reality we call God, we must never
> consider ourselves strangers toward any human
> being. Rather, we must bind ourselves to the task
> of sharing his experiences and try being of help to
> him.[56]

In loving God, we love creation, and in loving creation, we love God. Reverence for life compels us to become practical mystics who share in God's vision of Shalom which aims at everyone experiencing the possibility of abundance in body, mind, spirit, and relationships.

> Any profound view of the universe is mystic in that
> it brings men into spiritual relationship with the
> Infinite. The concept of reverence for life is ethical
> mysticism. It allows union with the infinite to be
> realized by ethical action.[57]

Union with the Infinite, with the Holy One, is the aim of life. Accordingly, mystical experiences lead to theological concepts, which are embodied in life-affirming ethical actions, embracing and supporting neighbors and strangers not only by intimate acts of compassion but also through acts of political transformation, seeking to universalize our compassion and support for the least of these, and enable everyone to experience the foundations for fulfilling their vocation as God's beloved children.

In the political realm, reverence for life challenges us to go beyond polarization to empathetic confrontation. One of the tragedies of the current political and social milieu is our lack of compassion toward those with whom we differ. Rather than attempting to understand what motivates other people's political and social positions, we condemn anyone who doesn't measure up to our ethical and political ideals. We often deny the worth of people with whom we fundamentally agree when they fail to use the current approved terminology to describe the marginalized or respond awkwardly to a marginalized person in their attempt to be helpful. Reverence for others honors their imperfect attempts to do the right thing, according to their—and our—current awareness and helps us grow through respect and relationship. It also recognizes our own fallibility and limited perspective.

It is important that I be clear on this point: I am speaking primarily to people of economic, social, and racial privilege like myself. Despite Thurman's belief that love can transform even the most intractable racism, I am not advising dispossessed and marginalized people to abandon their righteous anger and despair. They, too, are called to reverence of life and to bring wholeness to the political order, but the shape of their actions, like my own, depends on their unique political, social, and economic location. The privileged must, as Amos believed, move from apathy to empathy so that they can experience God's pain in the pain of the dispossessed. The privileged are challenged to recognize that those who have been marginalized have a right to affirm the holiness of their own lives and culture as a prelude to demanding equality in the social and political order, and before seeking unity with those of us who have been complicit in the injustice they have experienced. Despite our attempts to be just and empathetic, we must confess our own blindness and complicity in the evils that we protest.

Reverence for life and anger at injustice are not mutually exclusive. As noted earlier in this book, the prophetic tradition, whether embodied by Micah, Amos, Hosea, or Isaiah, challenges the self-interested behavior of the court preachers. The prophets know that the court preachers will reap what they sow in terms of their collusion with the wealthy to disenfranchise the poor. The Hebraic prophets' sermons are intended to cut these offenders to the core, to convict them of their white-collar violence, and challenge their smug religiosity. But the prophet's ultimate goal is a conversion of a heart, a contrite spirit that inspires the wealthy and their clergy sycophants to break down the walls of separation, recognize the relationship between their behavior and the suffering of God's children, and join in common cause to achieve God's vision of justice and community. As Micah asserts:

> He has told you, O mortal, what is good;
> and what does the LORD require of you
> but to do justice, and to love kindness,
> and to walk humbly with your God? (Micah 6:8).

Micah and his prophetic companions do not want to punish the wealthy, but to inspire them to justice-seeking that will deliver them from catastrophe. Like the prophets, we know there will be hell to pay for those who willfully destroy the environment, promote polarization, disparage the vulnerable, and inflame the fires of race. We also recognize, with the prophet, that our silence gives permission to those who perpetuate racism, economic injustice, and planetary destruction.

Reverence for life requires us to see the divine in those whose beliefs and actions we challenge. We need to see the holiness hidden beneath their fear and anger and desire to hold onto what they have, or what they want. We must understand they too are God's beloved children, despite their apparent racism, sexism, homophobia, and xenophobia. Without a doubt, reverencing such people seems almost impossible at times! Our anger is too great. The trauma they inflict on others is too painful. Their language and politics pushes all our emotional buttons and we want to fight back either with words or actions. We are tempted to hatred ourselves, described earlier in the words of the psalmist, well worth repeating as an antidote to our own polarization:

> O that you would kill the wicked, O God,
> and that the bloodthirsty would depart from me—
> those who speak of you maliciously,
> and lift themselves up against you for evil!
> Do I not hate those who hate you, O LORD?
> And do I not loathe those who rise up against you?
> I hate them with perfect hatred;
> I count them my enemies (Psalm 139:19-22).

But, then, like the psalmist, we are reminded that there is a deeper reality residing in ourselves and those whose behaviors lead us to believe they are in some way less than human.

Search me, O God, and know my heart;

test me and know my thoughts.

See if there is any wicked way in me,

and lead me in the way everlasting (Psalm 139:23-24).

I quote Psalm 139 for the second time in this text because this Psalm was especially inspiring to Howard Thurman in its recognition of the contrast between both our grandeur and our pettiness. It reminds us that awareness of our imperfections and limitations, and our temptation to hate in others what we are unconsciously practicing ourselves, is essential to prophetic healing. In recognizing that God knows us completely and loves us fully, we are given the opportunity to transcend our limited perspectives and begin to see the other as God sees her or him in all her or his woundedness and wonderfulness. Recognizing our own fallibility, we can affirm our political values without demeaning our opponents. In so doing, we open the door to a beloved community in which diversity leads to partnership and contrast leads to beauty.

A PRACTICE FOR PROPHETIC HEALING

Reverence for life begins right where we are with our own self-affirmation, based on God's presence in our own lives. Prayerfully contemplate these words from Jesus' Sermon on the Mount:

> You are the light of the world. A city built on a hill cannot be hid. No one after lighting a lamp puts it under the bushel basket, but on the lampstand, and it gives light to all in the house (Matthew 5:13–14).

After internalizing Jesus' words, you may choose to change them into an affirmation whose purpose is first to change your mind and then, after regular repetition, transform your whole attitude toward life. Some affirmations that I use based on this passage are:

> I am the light of the world.
> God's light shines through me.
> I let my light shine to give light to others.

Then, I turn this affirmation toward others with whom I interact; first, my family, friends, and associates, and then people whom I struggle to love. These affirmations are intended to inspire us to see them with the eyes of love, and promote feelings of unity despite our differences:

I look for light in those with whom I disagree ethically and politically.

> You are the light of the world.
> I look beyond your exterior to see your inner light.
> May your light shine to give healing light to the world.

Regularly pray for those with whom you live, seeing the light within them. Regularly pray for your nation's political leaders, looking beyond their rough exterior to see God's light bursting forth from its hiding place. In praying for our leaders, we create a "field of grace" that brings greater wisdom and positive energy to their lives. In prayer, we don't dictate the form of their behavior or how God's wisdom will transform their lives and liberate them from apathy, greed, or any other illness of the heart or spirit we may identify. Our prayers do not blunt our need to protest injustice wherever it occurs. We must let go of the outcome of our prayers. Our prayers may open a door of love in our hearts as much as in those for whom we pray, increasing the influx of divine compassion and guidance for the common good in either case. Together we may be awakened to God's voice in the cries of the poor and our duty to respond to suffering and justice in its many forms, including those injustices for which we bear responsibility.

CHAPTER NINE

PROPHETIC EMPATHY

The core of my preaching has always concerned itself
with the development of the inner resources needed
for creating a friendly world of friendly men . . . .
To me it was important that individuals who were
in the thick of the struggle for social change would
be able to find renewal and fresh courage
in the spiritual resources of the church.[58]

The theme of empathy is at the heart of Howard Thurman's spiritual vision and has been an underlying principle throughout this book. Without empathy, healthy social change will elude us. Hate and condescension will crowd out feelings of loving connection. The common ground necessary for social transformation requires us to be empathetic across political, social, and racial differences.

At the heart of prophetic healing is the affirmation that we are all connected in an intricate and dynamic fabric of relationships. In this fabric of life, the joys and sorrows of each affect the whole. Though often hidden and denied, the essential unity of humankind has its foundation in the biblical affirmation that humankind bears God's image. While scripture does not attempt to define exactly how the image of God manifests in humankind—and with good reason, since too-precise definitions, whether in doctrine, anthropology, or politics, serve more often to exclude than include—at the very least the biblical understanding of *imago dei* means that there is a trace of divinity in every human being that can never be defaced by our behavior or others' attitudes toward us. This trace of divinity ideally inspires respect and empathy amid the varieties of race, culture, talent, religion, and place of origin that make up the human family.

In contrast to God's vision of unity, many of us live in political, religious, ethnic, racial, and sexual silos, in which we are joined as much by common hates as common identities. Indeed, one of the challenges in American politics today is that people have vastly different world views or ways of interpreting reality. Within the silos are our friends, outside are our enemies. Such sorting of humans into distinct "in" and "out" groups, exacerbated by the phenomenon of "alternative facts" and demagogic political and media spokespersons, makes differentiating and defeating the primary goal of our endeavors.

Others' life experiences and feelings are of little consequence if the goal of relationships involves winning an argument, proving the inferiority of another, or disregarding her or his perspective on life. In a world at war, those who differ from us are implicitly labeled as needing to be beaten, even eradicated, despite rhetorical protestations of "love your neighbor" or "God is love." They may even be identified as agents of Satan, unpatriotic, or utterly bereft of compassion and truth, as a Facebook friend of mine's comment suggested in relation to those who opposed his political viewpoint.

We become afraid of otherness because to admit that our neighbor's world view has some validity might threaten the validity of our own world view, whether in our political positions, our interpretations of scripture, or our opinions on any number of issues. It is impossible to have empathy when we fear that recognizing the value of another person's race, religious perspective, political viewpoint, or life experience puts our own identity and self-affirmation at risk.

As a child, Howard Thurman experienced what happens when empathy is absent in a person or community. Recall the incident when the young child pricked him with a hat pin and was astounded when he let out a shriek. When he cried out, the girl responded, "O Howard, that didn't hurt you. You can't feel."[59] This youthful experience shaped Thurman's approach to relational healing in the years to come.

"You can't feel!" Where would a four-year-old learn such a demeaning and hateful idea? Every child is born, as Celtic theologian Pelagius asserts, revealing God's presence. Young children seldom see race or sexual identity as a threat. Her lack of empathy was not merely the narcissistic self-centeredness appropriate to a young child; it was part of her inheritance of America's original sin of slavery and racism by which certain people were designated as subhuman chattel and resources to support others' way of life. She unconsciously adopted the racism of her parents and community. Throughout history, many cultures have designated certain people or groups as less than human—and therefore perhaps incapable of feeling, or intelligent thought, or other vital human traits—as a result of the color of their skin, cultural behaviors, language, class, education, or other traits. The wealthy "cows of Bashan" of Israel and their husbands, denounced by the prophet Amos, may have thought themselves to be moral and upright—after all, they supported the temple's building fund and religious services—but their morality did not extend to affirming the value and recognizing the pain of poor farmers, widows, and orphans (Amos 4:1-23).

The disparity between the rich and the poor, bringing ruin to many households, really didn't matter to the wealthy and powerful because "they" aren't like us, they don't have our values, education, and importance in the world. Their pain isn't important, for they do not share our full humanity. Their poverty and social standing may even be deserved, the result of laziness and immorality. The elite and wealthy of Israel were afraid that if they altered their economic system to ensure all receive justice, their accustomed way of life and sense of superiority would be at risk. I suspect they justified the gap between their wealth and other's poverty with a rationalization similar to that of today's business and political decision-makers: "It's nothing personal, after all, it's just business. It's how the system works. We know best what is good for society. If we take care of our own, and everyone follows our lead, then everyone who deserves success will receive it."

Today, only the most demagogic politicians are so blunt in their prejudice, at least publicly, about the humanity of people of other races, political viewpoints, or sexual identities. It is commonplace for our fellow citizens or people from other countries to be demeaned in the public arena. In politics and society, the poor must earn our support by their hardworking obsequiousness; their ethics and morality are always suspect by the balanced budget police. In contrast, the wealthy, whether their politics are liberal or conservative, are seldom required to justify their wealth or the tax reforms and subsidies that fill their pockets while social programs are reduced. After all, "they earned their wealth" even if they inherited it; it's their money and it shouldn't go to slackers, such as welfare mothers, the working poor, or people with mental or physical health issues that drive them to bankruptcy or homelessness.

Sadly, much of this unempathetic self-justification, of course, goes back to the scriptures that are employed by the privileged to suggest that poverty is the result of immorality or sloth or negative thinking while wealth is a sign of righteousness or hard work or positive thinking, and that those who differ from us belong to the "lost" and "unsaved." Nothing, of course, is further from the truth, as Jesus and the author of Job note. The rich and the poor, the righteous and unrighteous, are on the same spiritual and social footing. The sun shines and the rain falls on the good and bad alike (Matthew 5:45). Often misfortune, whether caused by random events, a health crisis, the behavior of one's parents, or social injustices such as slavery and racism, is the primary source of poverty and marginalization. In my own soul searching, I have come to realize that while I don't employ these phrases, these justifications, I am often complicit in the injustices of our economic and social order. If I fail to see my own subtle injustice, I separate myself, judging as immoral those who do not share my values and political positions. Confession of our own sense of superiority is essential to reconciling with those whose economic and social practices I challenge.

Empathy is the spiritual child of reverence. Empathy emerges when we discover the holiness of everyone. We would do well to see one another in terms of the wisdom of the geode. Beneath the rough, even ugly exterior, the geode hides something of great beauty. Beneath the guise of poverty, ignorance, distrust, fear, addiction, and all other human flaws, God's countenance is waiting to shine forth. Empathy is a choice, an expansion of our imagination that inspires behaviors that affirm the validity of otherness. Empathy becomes a reality when we leave our siloes and meet people face to face in all their diversity. In such moments, we listen to their stories, feel their pain, and honor their dreams. Difference, then, has the potential of leading to the affirmation of contrast—similar to appreciating the many colors on the rainbow, each with its own unique hue and gift—rather than distance and division. In empathetic relationships, we pause, notice, and then respond, out of a sense of appreciation for the divine spark beneath the contrasts we so often see in others.

Empathetic relatedness is grounded in the interplay of vision and humility. We train our eyes to see, beneath the bloviation and braggadocio, the anger and fear, the geodic exteriors of those with whom we contend. We look for their noblest intentions, even if at times the goodness of their intentions is difficult to perceive. We also work to recognize our own blind spots and moral and spiritual limitations and the limitations of our perspectives, recognizing our own actions may not always spring from our best selves and our good intentions may not be obvious to others.

Empathy doesn't promote acceptance of violent behavior, racism, homophobia, misogyny, bullying, alternative "facts," or policies that promote injustice and alienation. It may, in fact, lead to greater activism on behalf of those whose humanity is menaced by these threats. Jesus was empathetic with his opponents, despite his condemnation of their injustice. His tears over Jerusalem were for the powerful as well as the poor (Matthew 23:37-39). Empathetic spirituality enables us to confront unacceptable behaviors directly while looking for the possibility of common ground in the spark of divinity within us and within them.

To my knowledge, Howard Thurman and Will Campbell never met. But, I am sure that they shared a sense of God's never-ending rainbow love, inclusive of humankind in all its wondrous messiness. Will Campbell was a social progressive, the only white person who was present at the founding of the Southern Christian Leadership

Conference in 1957. His unique style made him the inspiration for Rev. Will B. Dunn in Doug Marlette's comic strip, *Kudzu*. When black students went to attend Arkansas' Little Rock High School in 1957, he was among the white ministers who escorted them past angry white protesters. Years later, Campbell scandalized many of his "liberal" friends by practicing what he called a "ministry of reconciliation," holding weddings and funerals in his Tennessee log cabin for whites and blacks—civil rights activists and racists—alike. "We are all bastards, but God loves us anyway," Rev. Campbell would say. "He often got taunted because he was a pastor to the Ku Klux Klan," said civil rights leader and United Methodist Rev. James Lawson. "He was on the human side, no matter what human. He loved all humans in the great spectrum of life." Writer John Edgerton stated that "he had a keen sense of how unique it was to come out of darkest Mississippi into the larger world and realize that the rest of the world was as screwed up as Mississippi." When a reporter asked him why he attended the trial of one of his parishioners, a former imperial wizard of the KKK who murdered a grocer who sold food to blacks, Campbell retorted, "Because I'm a Christian, Goddammit!"[60] Both Thurman and Campbell believed that all people are God's people and, to quote Will Campbell, "If you're gonna love one, you've got to love 'em all."[61]

That's the meaning of empathy. To sense an original wholeness beneath the obvious sin, to look for the emotions that underlie negative behaviors, and to recognize our own imperfections—the log in our own eye—when we seek to correct the sins of others (Matthew 7:3). In so doing, as theologian Reinhold Niebuhr suggests, we confront the truth in our neighbor's falsehood and the falsehood in our own truth. Then, in the interplay of humility and affirmation, we can begin the long process of personal and political healing.

A PRACTICE FOR PROPHETIC HEALING

In the spirit of empathy, take time to pray for all those from whom you feel alienated. While these days most of us are siloed in our affinity groups, we may need to explore ways to encounter friends and relatives who differ from us religiously and spiritually. I make it a point to have respectful dialogues with one pastor whose conservative political viewpoints contrast with my progressive politics. I affirm areas where we agree in terms of personal and political practices and note where we differ in a civil manner. We seldom agree but we respect each other.

If you have the opportunity to dialogue with someone whose political viewpoints diverge from your own, and this is best done in person, take time to pay attention, listening to their words before voicing your objections, trying to discern their concerns lying beneath what may appear to you as knee jerk reactions. Let go of the need to be "right," even if you are strongly committed to your position, so that you can "hear" them from the heart as well as head. Ask them to share their viewpoints and their fears on issues of disagreement. Feel free to share your own vision *without judgment on theirs*. Try to discern one place where you can meet on common ground or one action you can do together. You may not agree on policy matters related to governmental support of people in need, but you may choose to volunteer together at a soup kitchen or spend a day hammering nails or painting at a Habitat for Humanity build.

CHAPTER TEN

DEEP SPIRIT: PROPHETIC CONTEMPLATION

The religious experience is defined as a dynamic encounter between man and God through the experience of prayer and human suffering. All this has to do with the inwardness of religion. The outwardness of religion is examined in terms of the impact of the religious experience itself on the individual nervous system, thus altering ingrained behavior patterns as the new life takes hold and spreads its influence through all the living.[62]

Several years ago I was interviewed to be senior pastor of one of the flagship churches of my denomination. I had heard that the pulpit committee, responsible for calling the new pastor, was split on the type of pastor needed to move the congregation forward. The church was socially active, participating in and financing inner city projects, affordable housing, and human rights initiatives. The church also has quarterly spiritual life retreats, a meditation group, and yoga classes. In the course of my interview, the issue of the relationship of activism and spirituality came up and for several minutes I observed the pulpit committee engaged in a heated conversation about which approach was most central to the life of the church.

Many people still maintain an artificial dualism between spirituality and social activism. They assume that spirituality is primarily related to the inner life and almost always eventuates in a mystical withdrawal from society. They believe that experiences of self-transcendence and non-attachment prized by mystics and spiritual seekers draw them away from the maelstrom of political decision-making, social involvement, and planetary survival.

Conversely, many spiritually oriented people assume social activists are so concerned with practical issues of economics, equality, and human rights that they have little time for their inner lives. In their estimation, social activists believe that individual transformation is solely the result of changing the political and economic circumstances of people's lives. These critics of what they believe to be spiritually bereft social activism assert that most political involvement exacerbates the polarization and violence of our current social context. They observe hateful comments made by both sides about abortion, gun ownership, health care, foreign policy, and many other debates. They cite the many examples of revolutionaries whose behavior resembles their oppressors once they gain power. Critics charge that social activists fail to see the holiness of those with whom they contend, and thus write off any possibility of change or common ground between people of contrasting political positions.

Although these criticisms relate to certain mystics and social reformers, they tend to perpetuate an unnecessary dualism between time and eternity, body and spirit, and action and contemplation. Truly holistic spirituality affirms the earth in all its wondrous complexity and sees healing people and institutions as essential to authentic spirituality. Prophets care about our spirits as well as our social context, while social activists often recognize the impact of social change on personal values and spiritual hungers. Truly life-supporting social change recognizes the need for humility as well as protest, and the hope that people and policies can be transformed. Authentic social change promotes, as Howard Thurman notes, the basic quality of life necessary for widespread experiences of creativity, beauty, and spiritual growth among people of all races, sexual identities, and economic classes—of any kind of human difference. Society must change, as Thurman asserts, so that all may have the opportunity to experience the fullness of human life, body, mind, spirit, and relationships. This is the place where mysticism and social action intersect.

While Thurman admits that some mystics and activists fit the previously noted caricatures, he strongly contests such dualistic thinking in the relationship of spirituality and the body politic. Thurman would, no doubt, approve of the statement carved on a bench at Kirkridge Retreat Center in Bangor, Pennsylvania, "Picket and pray." He would also remind us of the long history of contemplative activists, such as Quakers George Fox, John Woolman, and his mentor Rufus Jones; prophet for the poor Dorothy Day; civil rights champion Martin Luther King, Jr.; peacemaker Dag Hammarskjold; and non-violent resister and liberator Mahatma Gandhi. He knew firsthand of Martin Luther King, Jr.'s deep prayer life and its impact on the long march toward freedom and equality for African Americans. Thurman was well aware of biblical examples of prophetic activism: Elijah finding divine guidance in the still, small voice; Isaiah receiving his calling in encounter with the Holy One in the temple; Amos responding to the voice of God illuminating the experience of the poor and challenging him to preach for social and economic justice; and Moses inspired by a burning bush to speak truth to power for the liberation of the Hebrews. Thurman affirmed Jesus' blend of prayer and action, and the missional power he received from times of silent contemplation. Out of their private encounters with the Holy One, each of these prophetic reformers was inspired to transform their societies to reflect God's vision of Shalom.

Indeed, people of faith, in the spirit of Thurman's own work, are realizing that what the world needs most today are contemplative activists who join the meditative listening of Mary with the lively activism of Martha. Thurman gives us a vision of holistic social trans-formation but does not explicitly provide practices for contemplative activism. Perhaps, he realized that religious experience begins, as Alfred North Whitehead observed, with solitariness, and that our unique spiritual experiences are often the catalyst for entering the maelstrom of politics and social change. Further, Thurman asserts that the mystic's initial inspiration to make a commitment to prophetic healing and contemplative activism is their sense of God's creative energy and wisdom flowing through all things and localizing itself in the uniqueness of human experience in terms of the *imago dei*, the image and incarnation of divine wisdom in each individual human that transcends all of our social distinctions and prejudices.

A contemporary of Howard Thurman, the French mystic-activist Simone Weil, saw the heart of prayer as paying attention. Behold, you are on holy ground! Behold, God's child stands before you: proud and arrogant, humiliated and abused, claiming privilege and receiving no consideration, healthy and beautiful and broken and disfigured and forgotten. Take off your shoes, bow down, and give reverence to God's presence disguised in human flesh: your flesh, your enemy's flesh, your beloved's flesh, the flesh of the powerful and the flesh of the dispossessed. Namaste! Opponents though we are, the divine in me recognizes and reveres the divine in you!

The prophetic healer embodies Jesus' Sermon on the Mount, Mahatma Gandhi's satyagraha ("soul force"), and Martin Luther King, Jr.'s non-violent resistance to social injustice. All of these emerge from a deep commitment to contemplation and imaginative prayer. In experiencing God in moments of stillness, we discover that same reality deep down in all people. We experience the image of God in the Roman legions, pharisaic legalists, British imperialists, European slave traders, liberated slaves, civil rights activists, and southern white supremacists. In quiet moments of solitude, we go both deep and wide. We go deep to recognize the divine within, experiencing the divinity we share with all people, and go wide in self-transcending hospitality and inclusion.

Moments of solitude come in many forms. For some solitude involves regular times of contemplation. I begin the day with a time of meditation, usually about twenty to thirty minutes, then take some time for writing, before going out for a prayer walk in my neighborhood. My neighborhood is a local Cape Cod beach, and during that meditative walk, I breathe in the beauty of the environment, make spiritual affirmations, and pray for people in need, including the wider world of politicians and national leaders. I take a moment to pray for the president, even when I may have serious problems with his behavior or policies. I pause during my top-of-the-hour viewing of cable news to pray for guidance and the ability to see the holiness in those with whom I disagree. I pray for a calm spirit to confront injustice with a spirit of justice to all involved. Others pray with their eyes open, catching glimpses of divinity amid the fray. They look for something of God within the personalities they see on cable news and at local political and governmental gatherings. These more extroverted contemplatives desire that their inner lives and political involvements be in synch.

Throughout his public ministry Thurman taught his congregants to contemplate scripture and other devotional passages. In worship services he often invited congregants to listen to a passage, letting it simmer, and then meditate on its meaning for their lives. Similar to the Benedictine practice of holy reading, or *lectio divina*, Thurman's meditative practice enables a scripture or contemplative reading to take root and shape our inner lives and outer behaviors. Such "centering moments" deepen our relationship with God and connect us at the spiritual level with all creation. Despite our differences, we discover our essential unity as God's beloved children.

Prophetic healing requires us to be in touch with what Thurman described as the deep river of God's Spirit. Flowing through us are the waters of justice and the breath of life. God's waters of justice join us with oppressor and oppressed alike, cleanse our spirits from hatred and violence, and allow us to protest in prayerful ways, honoring the divinity in those whom it seems are most defaced by injustice and violence. Remembering that God's Spirit moves freely through all things, every breath joins us with creation in all its wondrous and challenging diversity (John 3:8). In such moments of joining, we become participants in the prayer of creation and contact the deeper rhythms moving through every life.

We cannot be fully responsible for the transformation of political leaders and those who fan the flames of racism, sexism, and intolerance. But we can address them from a place of unity and calm. We can protest their injustice while recognizing our own fallibility. We can challenge policies that promote poverty and alienation while praying for those who promote such policies. In so doing, our activism is spirit-filled and persistent, and brings healing to the world.

A PRACTICE FOR
PROPHETIC HEALING

In this practice, we turn to an abbreviated version of the Benedictine practice of *lectio divina*, or holy reading, often utilized in Thurman's meditations at the Church of the Fellowship of All Peoples in San Francisco, California, and the Marsh Chapel at Boston University. This simplified version involves: 1) reading or listening to a text, whether spiritual or biblical in nature, reading it over two to three times silently or orally, 2) taking time for the words to soak in through a few minutes dedicated to silence, 3) listening for a word or phrase that emerges as God's address to you, 4) praying with that word or phrase, asking how it relates to your life and what action would appropriately follow from it, and 5) closing with a prayer that you live throughout the day ahead in the spirit of the insights you've received.

Here is one useful reading, the well-known Bible passage involving Mary, Martha, and Jesus:

> Now as they went on their way, he entered a certain village, where a woman named Martha welcomed him into her home. She had a sister named Mary, who sat at the Lord's feet and listened to what he was saying. But Martha was distracted by her many tasks; so she came to him and asked, "Lord, do you not care that my sister has left me to do all the work by myself? Tell her then

to help me." But the Lord answered her, "Martha, Martha, you are worried and distracted by many things; there is need of only one thing. Mary has chosen the better part, which will not be taken away from her" (Luke 10:38-42).

Let the word and wisdom of God soak in. As you spiritually encounter the passage, in what ways are you like Martha? In what ways are you like Mary? What do you need to find balance between action and contemplation in your spiritual life and social action? What next steps do you need to take to be faithful to God's calling in your life? Prayerfully commit your insights to God's blessing.

CHAPTER ELEVEN

SOMETHING BEAUTIFUL FOR GOD

By some amazing but vastly creative
spiritual insight the slave undertook
the redemption of a religion
that the master had profaned in his midst.[63]

Howard Thurman joined mysticism and social transformation. He was keenly aware of God's creative wisdom as the animating force in all things. God's voice whispers through the wind, roars in the thunder, and chants in the waves. An oak tree reveals God's creative wisdom and so does the color purple. In the spirit of the hymn "This Is My Father's World," from childhood onward, Thurman was able to "hear God's voice everywhere." Thurman's vision of an enchanted world gave him hope for social change and the healing of the wounds inflicted through America's sin of slavery and the realization of a friendly world of friendly people.

The moral arc is long, but it bends toward justice, as Theodore Parker asserted. As the deepest reality of all creation, human and non-human, God will outlast those who promote hatred, racism, sexism, and ecological destruction. Right now, at this moment, the ever-present, ever-active God is whispering in the ears of the privileged and the oppressors, "Hear my voice in the cries of the poor and dispossessed; hear my plea in the pain of our non-human companions; hear my challenge in thunder and storm. Change your life, so others can also hear my voice. Change your priorities so that all experience liberty and justice." The hymn writer Maltbie Babcock captured this same spirit of hope amid challenge:

> This is my Father's world.
> O let me ne'er forget
> that though the wrong seems oft so strong,
> God is the ruler yet.
> This is my Father's world:
> why should my heart be sad?
> The Lord is King; let the heavens ring!
> God reigns; let the earth be glad![64]

Thurman challenges us to be mystical activists. We can be hopeful, despite the long and often ponderous arc of social transformation, because God's call is unceasing and constant. The evils we face are strong, but the darkness can never conquer God's light (John 1:5).

When I think of Thurman's vision of prophetic healing, I am drawn to Mother Teresa of Calcutta's calling to do "something beautiful for God" as she ministered to the dying outcasts on Calcutta's streets. The saint of Calcutta saw God's presence beneath the disguises of untouchability, social ostracism, sickness, and poverty. Doing something beautiful for God is also our calling as we seek to be God's partners in prophetic healing, taking on our role as God's companions in healing the world.

Prophetic healing takes place in two primary ways, as Thurman knew. First, God's prophetic power is found in the healing of personal relationships through individual face-to-face encounters that cross barriers of race, gender, ethnicity, politics, and economics. Second, it leads us to seek how we can have a role in the healing of society's institutions, moving us to go from apathy to empathy in public policies, which shape our lives for good or ill. Inspired by a sense of God's intimacy, we discover that every moment can be a healing moment. Every encounter can enable us to move from alienation and misunderstanding to reconciliation and partnership.

In the interplay of personal and relational well-being, God's prophetic healing inspires institutional transformation, which in turn transforms individuals. No person stands alone. All of us are shaped by social structures and governmental policies. While their words were often strident and threatening to the wealthy, powerful, and privileged, the Hebraic prophets' apparent anger was inspired by an inclusive love that embraced not only the poor, who require a preferential option in social policy because of their vulnerability, but also the powerful who need a conversion of heart and transformation of values to truly hear the voice of God. Prophetic warnings appeared harsh to their intended audience, but just as harsh are the words of Jesus:

> For those who want to save their life will lose it, and those who lose their life for my sake, and for the sake of the gospel, will save it. For what will it profit them to gain the whole world and forfeit their life?" (Mark 8:35–36).

Like the healer Jesus, the prophets' hearts are filled with grief as they ponder the fate of the unjust as well as the unjustly treated. Jesus' care includes oppressor and oppressed alike. As he gazed upon the holy city of Jerusalem, Jesus mourned its waywardness:

> Jerusalem, Jerusalem, the city that kills the prophets
> and stones those who are sent to it! How often have
> I desired to gather your children together as a hen
> gathers her brood under her wings, and you were
> not willing!" (Matthew 23:37).

One of the greatest challenges for those who seek to be prophetic healers in our time is to shed the sense of powerlessness. In a recent study group at our church, one of the members, a dedicated Christian woman active in responding to homelessness in our community, confessed "there is so much going on and I feel impotent to do anything to change the world. What can I do to change the world, locally or institutionally?" As those around the circle nodded their heads, she realized that she was not alone in her feelings of powerlessness. As they say on Cape Cod, my boat is so small and the sea is so great! We feel dwarfed by the immensity of ongoing social problems, not to mention the moment by moment "breaking news," which always seems to be negative, that confronts us in the media.

Howard Thurman knew what it was like to feel powerless, but he came to believe that every person, including those whose backs are against the wall due to centuries of social injustice and racism, can do something to change the world. This mustard seed faith, essential to Jesus' ministry, challenges those of us with privilege to go beyond hand wringing to spiritual activism and those at the margins to join prayer and protest for the greater glory of God and the well-being of the planet. In speaking to young pastors, Thurman noted:

> It is your particular task as preachers, my young
> friends, to call attention again and again to the fact
> that something more than one's country is at stake
> every day, every moment of the day. God is at stake

in everything that every man does. There is a sharp
pointed urgency in living every day. Each man, be
he high or low, rich or poor, learned or unlearned,
sick or well, every man lives under the Divine
Scrutiny.[65]

"God is at stake." Will we choose for God's Shalom or greed and
injustice? Will our love embrace our children's unborn children or
will we focus on short-term profit and heedless consumerism? Will
we see God in the stranger or erect walls of fear and hate to keep out
those who differ from us? According to Thurman, each day is an act
of faith, calling us toward the values we affirm and our vocation to
live these values out one moment, encounter, and day at a time. For
most of us, the world is not saved by doing one great thing, but by
doing many small, otherwise ordinary things, with great love for God
and our fellow humans.

As impotent as we may feel—even if perhaps we are among
those privileged with education and economic sufficiency—we can
raise the spiritual temperature wherever we find ourselves. We have
resources to be God's companions in the process of creative transformation in our communities and nation. We can make a phone call
to a representative. We can send letters to the White House. We can
collect petitions for a cause we believe in whether environmental,
economic, or racial. We can speak words of welcome and appreciation to people from other nations, grateful for their commitment
to our country. We can march with women protesting harassment
and discrimination, with those experiencing poverty in the "poor
peoples' march," and high school kids "marching for our lives." We
can stand quietly with those who are unjustly treated. And, if we are
physically limited or cannot march for some other reason, we can

pray! The world is transformed by prayers of believing people. Our prayers radiate across the universe, creating energy fields of love, justice, and healing. One simple act can bring self-esteem to a child, reconciliation to an opponent, healing to a broken spirit, and affirmation to an outcast.

When it comes down to it, prophetic healing is ultimately about the promotion of beauty in everyday life and social relationships. It is about creating the conditions for personal transformation, intellectual growth, and healthy family life so that people might experience their own personal beauty, the beauty of loving relationships, and the beauty of the earth. The path to healing occurs one step at a time, and one act at a time. In the spirit of Jesus' parable of the lost sheep, the ninety-nine sheep require the return of the one lost sheep in order to be whole. When you save one child, you save the universe, and when you convict one political leader of her or his heartlessness, you transform the world and bring healing to this good earth.

A SPIRITUAL PRACTICE FOR PROPHETIC HEALING

I conclude this text by inviting you to make a commitment to cultivating a sense of beauty. Some spiritual guides suggest that the world is saved by beauty. Prophetic healing brings beauty to individual lives and institutions. The Navajo blessing prayer affirms, "With beauty all around me, I walk." We are surrounded by beauty, yet we are often oblivious. Let us begin by opening our senses to the beauty of the earth. Then, prayerfully, let us ask for ways we can promote beauty in our world. Beauty, as a theological concept, joins spirituality and social action. We can create structures of peace and justice so people can experience greater beauty in their lives. Injustice, poverty, intolerance, and bullying stunt the imagination and spirits of both oppressor and oppressed. Justice-seeking brings beauty to the earth.

As you act throughout the day, commit yourself to becoming a prophetic healer. At each juncture of the day, take time to ask the question: Does this act contribute to bringing beauty to the world? Will this action add to the pain and ugliness of life? In all things seek to do something beautiful for God.

We are not responsible for the outcome of our actions or how others respond to our best efforts. But, in this holy moment, we can be faithful to God and bring healing to this good earth.

Howard Thurman speaks of our lives as a holy adventure. We have work to do. The future of our nation and the planet is in the balance. We need prophets and we also need healers. We yearn for prophets whose prayerful protest against injustice and ecological destruction unite rather than divide and heal rather than harm. We must commit to becoming prayerful protesters ourselves, whose vision of a friendly world, God's world of Shalom, inspires us to claim our vocation as God's prophetic healers of this good earth.

NOTES

INTRODUCTION

1. Howard Thurman, *Deep Is the Hunger* (Richmond, IN: Friends United Press, 1964), 121.

2. Ibid., 86-87.

CHAPTER ONE

3. Howard Thurman, *The Mood of Christmas and Other Celebrations* (New York: Harper and Row, 1973), 23.

4. Martin Luther King, Jr., *A Knock at Midnight* (New York: Warner Books, 1998), 65.

5. Abraham Lincoln, *Complete Works of Abraham Lincoln* (Open Road Media, New York, 2017), 27.

6. Martin Luther King, Jr., *A Knock at Midnight* (New York: Warner Books, 1998), 76.

7. Martin Luther King, Jr., *A Testament of Hope* (New York: Harper One, 2003), 220.

8. Howard Thurman, *The Growing Edge* (Richmond, IN: Friends United Press), 180.

CHAPTER TWO

9. Howard Thurman, *Deep Is the Hunger* (Richmond, IN: Friends United Press, 1964), 44.

CHAPTER THREE

10. Howard Thurman, *With Head and Heart: The Autobiography of Howard Thurman* (New York: Harcourt and Brace, 1979), 9.

11. Ibid., 11-12.

12. Howard Thurman, *With Head and Heart: The Autobiography of Howard Thurman* (New York: Harcourt and Brace, 1979), 7.

13. Ibid., 226.

14. Ibid., 6.

15. Ibid., 21.

16. Ibid., 16.

17. Howard Thurman, *The Courage to Hope: From Black Suffering to Human Redemption* (Boston: Beacon Press, 1999), 22.

18. Howard Thurman, *Deep River and the Negro Spiritual Speaks of Life and Death* (Richmond, IN: Friends United Press, 1996), 11.

19. Maya Angelou, *The Complete Poetry of Maya Angelou* (New York: Random House, 2015), 261.

CHAPTER FOUR

20. Howard Thurman, *With Head and Heart: The Autobiography of Howard Thurman* (New York: Harcourt, Brace and Company, 1979), 268-269.

21. Ibid., 24.

22. Ibid., 36.

23. Ibid., 49.

24. Ibid., 140.

25. Howard Thurman, *Jesus and the Disinherited* (Boston: Beacon Press, 1976), 67.

26. Howard Thurman, *With Head and Heart: The Autobiography of Howard Thurman* (New York: Harcourt, Brace and Company, 1979), 114.

27. Ibid., 114.

28. Ibid., 134.

29. Ibid., 265-266.

CHAPTER FIVE

30. Luther E. Smith, *Howard Thurman: Mystic as Prophet* (Richmond, IN: Friends United Press, 2007), 35.

31. Howard Thurman, *Mysticism and Social Action: Lawrence Lectures and Discussions with Dr. Howard Thurman* (London: IARF, 2014), Kindle Location 109.

32. Ibid., 113-114.

33. Ibid., 116-117.

34. Ibid., 120-121.

35. Ibid., 177-179.

36. Alfred North Whitehead, *The Function of Reason* (Boston: Beacon Press, 1969), 4, 8.

37. Ibid., 235-236.

38. Ibid., 244-245.

39. Ibid., 249-251.

40. Ibid., 270-274.

41. Ibid., 335-337.

CHAPTER SIX

42. Luther Smith, *Howard Thurman: Mystic as Prophet* (Richmond, IN: Friends United Press, 2007), 127.

43. Howard Thurman, *Jesus and the Disinherited* (Boston: Beacon Press, 1976), 2.

44. Ibid., 34.

45. Ibid., 23.

46. Ibid., 33.

47. Ibid., 39.

48. Ibid., 79, 81.

49. Ibid., 88.

50. Howard Thurman, *A Strange Freedom: The Best of Howard Thurman on Religious Experience and Public Life* (Boston: Beacon Press, 1998), 300.

CHAPTER SEVEN

51. Ibid., 248.

52. Howard Thurman, *The Search for Common Ground* (Richmond, IN: Friends United Press, 1986), 2-3.

53. Ibid., 104.

54. Ibid., 41.

CHAPTER EIGHT

55. Howard Thurman, *Deep River and the Negro Spiritual Speaks of Life and Death* (Richmond, IN: Friends United Press, 1975), 12.

56. Albert Schweitzer, *Out of My Life and Thought: An Autobiography* (Baltimore: Johns Hopkins Press, 1990), 139-140.

57. Ibid., 237.

CHAPTER NINE

58. Howard Thurman, *With Head and Heart: The Autobiography of Howard Thurman* (New York: Harcourt, Brace and Company, 1979), 160.

59. Ibid., 12.

60. Randy Cassingham, "Will Campbell: Maverick Minister," from "This Is True," June 9, 2013 (http://www.honoraryunsubscribe.com/everyone/).

61. Peter Cooper, "Will Campbell: A Bootleg Preacher Who Tried to Love Them All", June 28, 2013. (https://www.tennessean.com/story/news/local/2017/03/01/campbell-bootleg-preacher-who-tried-love-them-all/98584950).

CHAPTER TEN

62. Howard Thurman, *With Head and Heart: The Autobiography of Howard Thurman* (New York: Harcourt, Brace and Company, 1979), 226-227.

CHAPTER ELEVEN

63. Howard Thurman, *Deep River and the Negro Spiritual Speaks of Life and Death* (Richmond, IN: Friends United Press, 1975), 36.

64. Maltbie Babcock, "This Is My Father's World," 1901 (https://hymnary.org/text/this_is_my_fathers_world_and_to_my).

65. Howard Thurman, *A Strange Freedom: The Best of Howard Thurman on Religious Experience and Public Life* (Boston: Beacon Press, 1998), 126.

BIBLIOGRAPHY

Angelou, Maya, *The Complete Poetry of Maya Angelou*. New York: Random House, 2015.

Epperly, Bruce, *The Mystic in You: Discovering a God-Filled World*. Nashville, TN: Upper Room Books, 2018.

King, Jr., Martin Luther. *A Knock at Midnight*. New York: Warner Books, 1998.

King, Jr., Martin Luther. *A Testament of Hope*. New York: Harper One, 2003.

Smith, Luther. *Howard Thurman: The Mystic as Prophet*. Richmond, IN: Friends United Press, 2007

Thurman, Howard. *The Centering Moment*. Richmond, IN: Friends United Press, 1984.

Thurman, Howard. *Deep Is the Hunger.* Richmond, IN: Friends United Press, 1978.

Thurman, Howard. *Deep River and the Negro Spiritual Speaks of Life and Death*. Richmond, IN: Friends United Press, 1996.

Thurman, Howard. *The Growing Edge*. Friends United Press, 2014.

Thurman, Howard. *Jesus and the Disinherited*. Boston: Beacon Press, 1976.

Thurman, Howard. *The Luminous Darkness*. Richmond, IN: Friends United Press, 2014.

Thurman, Howard. *The Mood of Christmas and Other Celebrations*, New York: Harper and Row, 1973.

Thurman, Howard. "Mysticism and Social Action: Lawrence Lectures and Discussions with Dr. Howard Thurman." London: International Association for Religious Freedom, 2014

Thurman, Howard. *The Search for Common Ground*. Richmond, IN: Friends United Press, 1986.

Thurman, Howard. *A Strange Freedom: The Best of Howard Thurman on Religious Experience and the Public Life*, Boston: Beacon Press, 2014.

Thurman, Howard. *With Head and Heart: The Autobiography of Howard Thurman*, New York: Harcourt and Brace, 1979.

BRUCE EPPERLY

Theologian, pastor, spiritual guide, author, and recognized leader in lay and pastoral faith formation, Bruce Epperly serves as Pastor at South Congregational Church, United Church of Christ, Centerville, Massachusetts, and professor in the D.Min. program at Wesley Theological Seminary. He has served on the faculties and administrative and chaplaincy roles at Georgetown University, Claremont School of Theology, Wesley Theological Seminary, and Lancaster Theological Seminary. Prior to coming to Cape Cod to serve as pastor of South Congregational Church, he served as Director of Continuing Education and Professor of Practical Theology at Lancaster Theological Seminary.

An ordained minister in the Christian Church (Disciples of Christ) and United Church of Christ, Dr. Epperly has written or co-written over fifty books in the areas of theology, spirituality, ministerial excellence and spiritual formation, scripture, and healing and wholeness, including *Become Fire: Guideposts for Interspiritual Pilgrims; The Mystic in You: Discovering a God-filled World; Finding God in Suffering: A Journey with Job; Process Theology: Embracing Adventure with God;* and *A Center in the Cyclone: Clergy Self-care for the 21st Century.* Bruce and Kate Epperly's co-written *Tending to the Holy: The Practice of the Presence of God in Ministry*, was selected as 2009 Book of the Year by the Academy of Parish Clergy. His most recent books include *Prophetic Healing: Howard Thurman's Vision of Contemplative Activism* and *God Online: A Mystic's Guide to the Internet.*

Dr. Epperly speaks regularly throughout North America on subjects such as: healing and wholeness, personal and congregational spiritual formation, process theology, ministerial spirituality and excellence, emerging Christianity, and contemporary movements in theology and spirituality. He has appeared on "Nightline," "ABC World News Tonight," and "PBS News Hour."